The Ruminations of Bing

Lines From My Forehead 3

Tim Harnden-Taylor

Published by Saron Publishing in 2019

Copyright © 2019 Tim Harnden-Taylor
All photos copyright © 2011-2019 Tim Harnden-Taylor
and
Anna Ross

All rights reserved

No part of this publication may be reproduced, stored in a retrieval system, or transmitted, in any form or by any means, without the prior permission in writing of the publisher, nor be otherwise circulated in any form of binding or cover other than that in which it is published and without a similar condition including this condition being imposed on the subsequent purchaser

ISBN-13: 978-1-9999871-8-3

Saron Publishers
Pwllmeyrick House
Mamhilad
Mon
NP4 8RG

www.saronpublishers.co.uk
info@saronpublishers.co.uk
Follow us on Facebook and Twitter

Also by Tim Harnden-Taylor

The Meanderings of Bing

The Ramblings of Bing

DEDICATION

For our dear friends near and far
May you always be blessed and
know how loved you are

CONTENTS

1	Introduction	11
2	There You Go, Bing	14
3	Found and Hounded Out and About	15
4	It's That Time of Year…Again	19
5	A Job Well Done	24
6	Time Marches On	27
7	Christmas	31
8	A Christmas Carol?	34
9	Just One More Stroll	37
10	April Blooming Showers…And Such!	40
11	Spotting The Eyes and Crossing The Teas	44
12	Seeing And Getting The Point	48
13	Spring?	51
14	Orchestrated Manoeuvres In The Bark	55
15	Henrys and Georges and Such	58
16	Brexits And Exits!	61
17	Somewhere In The Wood Of Brent	66
18	Stopped…For The Moment!	70
19	Life From 1-6…And So Forth	73
20	And For Those Of You Watching In Black And White	78
21	'The Thing Is, Ol' Wrinkly Chops'	81

22	The Art Of Dozing	83
23	Thoughts From France...But Of Home	86
24	It's A Var, Var Better Place That I Go To...	88
25	Angela Lansbury Will Never Know...	91
26	Birds Of A Feather	95
27	From Green Baize To Greenwood	99
28	Monks Have Habits...Bing Has Routines...	103
29	Sunday Morning Guests	106
30	Now Where Was I?	109
31	My Particular 'Woad' To Recovery!	112
32	It's All About Whether...The Weather Is...Whatever	115
33	Not Quite An O'Henry Tale	119
34	Food For Thought...And So Forth And Such Like	122
35	Blow, Blow, Thou Winter Wind!	127
36	Letting Sleeping Dogs...?	130
37	Dairylea & Pineapple Poll	133
38	To Sleep, Perchance To Dream	136
39	When It's Raining, It Must Be...Games Day!	138
40	One Hundred Not Out!	140
41	Pep Talks And Their Worth	142
42	The Missing Link...And Other Items	146
43	Now He Is Four	149
44	The Moving Pen Writes...	152
45	Scents and Sensibility	155

ACKNOWLEDGMENTS

Who'd have thought?

Folks, here we are about to head off for further moments regarding the Boy Bing and an old poop. The lad, who wanders over to 'Lyons' several times a week, seems to quite enjoy the company of a bumbling old codger and the routine we have settled very happily into.

I am told, when it comes to a strong-willed determination to train a hound and keep him on track, I am apparently not the shop for it! I find this a tad harsh. I might not have the heavy-handed manner of an over-officious chair and whip-toting lion tamer, but I feel that what I lack in overbearing threats, I more than make up for in subtle hints and the odd treat or two. ('Or three, guv.')

Once again, the wonderful Penny Reeves and Saron Publishers have dared to release more of The World of Bing for his many fans and those yet to discover these events, which mainly take place close to Old London Town, hard by the ancient forest of Epping.

I must thank our dear friend Barbara Read for suggesting the title, The Ruminations of Bing. This captures perfectly his thoughtful behaviour...and such. As the years toddle by, the lad has become very much a ruminator, dare I say, rather in the mould of a certain ol' poop.

The talented Anna Ross has supplied the photos, and sensibly has featured the lad rather than the non-

photogenic aged gent...'you lucky people'. (As another more famous TT* used to say!)

I am extremely lucky that Tom, Angela, an Arthur and the Hugo, still allow Bingo to spend time with me, along with the long-suffering Alison. Despite her protestations over the years, she has acquiesced to our sport watching from various comfy positions. Just between us, I've now stopped trying to emulate Bing by watching much of it from an upside-down position. Let's face it, I'm not a complete idiot. (Yet.)

Frankly, I regard you, our readers, as our dearest pals. We may not meet too often, if ever, but you are always with us when you take time to read a page or two and briefly join us in these 'episodes'.

Bless you all, always...

Tim & Bing...and such.

*Tommy Trinder

The Ruminations of Bing

Introduction

'Hi yer, guv.'

'Hello, Bing, just the chap I was looking for.'

'Strangely, I was looking for the snack tin.'

'Really?'

'Well, I know where it is but require the kind attention of a dear old gent and his ability to open it and pass two or three of the contents over.'

I receive such a delightfully open expression, not far short of saintliness, from the lad, I'm therefore inclined to believe he is not conning the easy touch, known as 'the guv'.

Suitably armed with his snacks, I attempt to continue my current quest.

'The thing is, Bing...'

'Yes, ol' poop?'

'Your publisher...'

'AND Christmas snack provider.'

'My, what a memory you have.'

'Cor, not half, guv, suppliers of extra treats and snacks come mighty high on the list of chaps like me.'

'Nevertheless, Bing, Penny has intimated that an update regarding you might be of interest.'

'Might, guv? Might?'

'Well, um, yes, Bing.'

Tim Harnden-Taylor

'There's no *might* about it, guv. When it comes to updates, I'm just the chap for it...and so forth.'

'Have you any words you wish to add that would be suitable for an introduction to volume 3?'

'How about...Dear reader, a book in your hand is worth snacks to a Bing.'

'I see.'

'Do you, guv? I wonder if you, as a mere pen-pusher, can grasp the literary pressures a hound of letters has to contend with?'

'M'mmmm.'

'I merely place such matters before you, old poop, in the hope that in future, when the snack tin is sought, it is because the muse is upon the brow of a certain hound, seated a mere whisker from you, guv.'

I receive a peering look, just to see if I've been taken in.

'You very nearly convinced me, Bing.'

'Well, it was worth a try. Was *muse* a tad too far?'

'Quite.'

'Well, I aim to *amuse,* guv.'

'That you most certainly do, Bing, you most definitely do.'

'Hurrah!'

So here it is - Volume 3 of Bing.

'And not before time, guv!'

'M'mmm.'

The Ruminations of Bing

Tim Harnden-Taylor

There You Go, Bing...

'Ah, yes, well, there you go, Bing.'

'Do I, guv?'

'Well...'

'And if I do go, where is it I'm going to?'

'The thing is, Bing...'

'Ye-eees?'

'The thing is, when I said *there you go,* I was merely observing that, in this case, *there you go* was merely an affirmation of your observation that I have a habit of talking to myself.'

'M'mmmm.'

'Therefore, I was, in this particular case, agreeing with you.'

'Well, guv, you hardly not agreed, eh?'

'Quite.'

Bing gave me a sweet smile and returned to the lounge.

For several moments, I stood in the hall, and having patted the top of my head, and left hand shirt pocket, I enquired of myself where the devil did I leave my glasses?

I froze. Had I just actually, yet again, spoken to myself?

As I tip-toed away, I heard...

'Yes, you did, guv.'

(Blast.)

Found And Hounded Out....And About!

Quite how the lad has got me out and about today I'm not sure.

Sadly, the view Alison has of me, is one of being a very easy touch when it comes to the Boy Bing. I fear there is more than a grain of truth in this.

Even so, I was quietly going about my 'non working day' morning routine. This entailed staring at the grass and wondering if I should give it a 'hoover', as Bing would say, or allow the daisies a day or two's more grace, before returning the lawn to green. (I use the term 'lawn' in its loosest sense...we are not talking bowling or golf green quality.)

I'd just poured a second or third cup of coffee and was about to give the odd 'spent' rose bloom the snip, when I heard a discreet cough behind me.

'Oh, hi, Bing, how you going?'

'On four legs as usual, guv.'

Tim Harnden-Taylor

He peered at me from under his fringe, and I'm not sure if he winked or I just imagined it. I decided to ignore the former, and as I wandered over to a rambling rose, he followed, taking a keen interest in a large potted plant whose name I forget, but Bing assures me is Keith.

'Keith?

'So, old poop, what sort of rose is that?'

'A rambling one.'

'And its name, oh, mighty oracle?'

I ignored any sense of irony in his voice and hunted for the tag generally sited at the bottom of such a plant.

'Ah, the label seems to have gone missing, Bing.'

'So, you don't know, guv?'

I blushed at the sound of incredulity in his voice.

'Ah, well, let me see, now...um, er...'

'I do believe I know – oh, label loser of Lyons.'

The Ruminations of Bing

(For those not in the know, Lyons is the name of our house...and yes, it is on a corner!)

'Really, Bing?'

'Certainly, guv, certainly.'

The silence was not 'golden' as I waited for the answer. Time passed, and I tried not to get impatient...eventually, I could stand it no longer...

'And so, what is it called?'

'Red.'

'Red?'

'Yes, guv, it's a red rose, or hadn't you noticed?'

'Well, um, yes, of course.'

'Yet its colour didn't nudge your ancient napper into blurting out the answer?'

'Well, of course, I knew it was red.'

'Was it really so difficult to impart that information, old codger?'

'No, you see, I thought you wanted to know its Latin name.'

'Oh, like Keith over there.'

'Bing, Keith is not a Latin name.'

'Well, don't tell him, guv, he'll be bitterly disappointed as his label clearly says his origins are Mediterranean in origin.'

'I see. I think.'

'Jolly good.'

I continued to deadhead and enjoy the early morning sun warming me as I worked on.

A short while later, I was seated in a garden chair, again contemplating the fate of the daisy heads as, innocently, they were all smiling in the sunshine.

'So, guv, why is the Red rose a rambler?'

'Well, you see, Bing, it rather likes to trundle over trellis, walls and such.'

'And so forth?'

'Yep.'

'What do they do over walls and such like?'

'Trundle.'

'Great, I don't mind if I do, guv.'

'What?'

'Well, it would be rude of me not to come with you for a trundle over walls and trellis and, more importantly, forest path!'

'But, but, but...'

'Never fear, old poop, I know where the lead is...come on!'

To be continued...possibly.

The Ruminations of Bing

It's That Time Of Year...
Again!

The Boy Bing is over at 'Lyons', spending the day with the old poop, who has 'broken up' for the Christmas holidays, and is at this moment adding the finishing touches to some decorations.

The lad has settled on a settee and is closely noting my efforts. I can feel he is simply bursting to ask me something but realises I'm at a crucial stage and the next few moments could either see me smile or grumble like Scrooge!

All is well, the branches are *in situ* and appear to be quite happy to stay there. I perch on a chair and take a slug of coffee.

A throat is cleared.

'Um...er, excuse me, guv, may I ask a question?'

This from Bing is very thoughtful. Generally he can quiz me endlessly about this, that and such like and so forth...but today he is noting all the preparations for the coming festive time and memories are stirring within the mysterious depths of his mind.

'What are you wondering about, Bing?'

'Well, guv, it's like this.'

The lad, having got my attention, rests a paw on my knee and looks very earnestly into my face.

'The thing is, old poop, I definitely seem to recall a time like this before, but I'm not sure quite what it's all about.'

I look into the earnest eyes and start to consider how deeply I should go into the Christmas story? Finally, I'm about to talk of Christmas, both temporal and spiritual, when the lad's hooter starts to gently twitch and within seconds, the nostrils are positively flaring with interest, and as if in agreement, the lad's tail has started to wag.

Why?

Well, into the lounge has come the smell of cooking. Cooking of a Christmassy type, thus the hound bit of Bing has snapped into action.

As I watch, I can see a look of deep thought trundling over the furrowed brow, and computer like, he is in the process

The Ruminations of Bing

of wandering around the various 'scent' areas within his mind, in search of a memory of this particular pong coming from the kitchen.

I try not to be impatient, as I'm rather relieved that, for the moment, I'm saved from explaining the ins and outs of Christmas and its various connotations.

The eyes are narrowing and the tail is beating gently as his inner 'hooter' wanders through the labyrinth that is the lad's memory. The steady drumming of tail on carpet becomes stronger, and I can see the seeker is slowly resurfacing from within with an answer!

'Crumbs, guv, it's time for ol' Daddy Christmas and so forth...'

'Correct!'

'Well I never and if I did, I'd forgotten, old poop!'

'Yes, lad, it's that time of year again...'

'Lummy, guv, crumbs and lummy again.'

The realisation of all that this particular time means is slowly working its way around his mind and he suddenly freezes and...

'Gulp, guv, oh dear, um...'

'Ye-e-e-s?'

'Well, I mean to say, cor, and here we are again and so forth and lummy and suchlike, flip and oops and what, what!'

'Are you okay, Bing?'

I am peered at from behind a shaggy brow.

'Well, I mean to say, I try and do my best and such but really, if ol' Pappy Christlemus is going to creep up on a chap and take him unawares and the like, well, a chap can't be perfect all the time...can he?'

Tim Harnden-Taylor

'Bing.'

'Yes, guv?'

'The thing about the jolly ol' gent in red is he realises that some folk aren't absolutely perfect.'

'I see. You mean, like you, guv?'

'Me?'

'Not that I don't think you are not um...er...'

'Let us not worry about me, Bing, it's certain chaps that need to be of the very best behaviour.'

'Lummy, guv.'

'Bing, taking all in all and by and large, by the whiskers on your chin and a long nose, I think once again you have managed to sidle through the "give this lad a treat or three" door, and should be okay for another year.'

'Hurrah!'

I am treated to a lap of honour around the lounge, finished off with a dive onto a settee...I do believe he even managed to click his heels as he landed on the cushions!

The Ruminations of Bing

I'm reliably informed by those that know, tomorrow Bing is off for a pre-Christmas wash, trim and brush-up...which will mean next time, you'll get a less shaggy dog story than usual...

...thanks, Bingo, for another 'interesting' year!!

Tim Harnden-Taylor

A JOB WELL DONE

'Well, Bing, I'm mighty pleased with that, the computer is back up and running!'

'I admire your confidence, guv, but I fear you are getting a tad over-excited too soon.'

'I'm aware you have a very low opinion of my computer skills, but I have been most meticulous and am confident you will be amazed with my efforts.'

The Ruminations of Bing

'As you know, guv, I'm only a hound, but is the screen supposed to roll every time you press Return?'

'Blast!'

'Cheer up, old wheezer, you did very well...considering.'

'Considering what, Bing?'

'Well, it's like this, guv...'

'When I peer into your left earhole, I can see the light coming through from your right!'

Tim Harnden-Taylor

'Don't despair, old poop, soon be Christmas...and such.'

'Hello, hello, hello...that new ginger cat is trundling about over the road.'

'WOOF!'

'Now that's a real gift, guv! Better crack the snack tin open, eh?'

The Ruminations of Bing

Time Marches On

'So, what's all that about, guv?'

It's the time when I wander about the house winding clocks and making sure all timepieces are approximately displaying the correct time.

I'm currently standing in front of the old Grandfather Clock and winding the time and then the chime. Strangely, whenever I do this, I think of the number of people over nearly 200 years, who've stood before it, doing the same thing. I'm just another person charged with this duty, and I hope many more will follow.

Job done, I check the date is right and move on.

'Well, Bing, each one of these "faces" tells us the time, which in turn, enables us to be aware of any timetable we might be running to.'

Immediately the lad rolls on his back and...

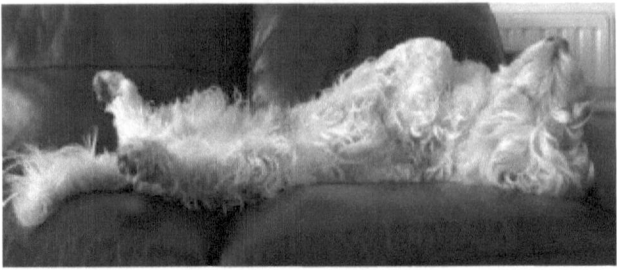

'Oh ha-ha-ha-ha-ha-ha...he-he-he...'

He peers at me through his fringe and attempts to straighten his face...

'It's no good, guv...ha-ha-ha-ha-ha-ha!'

'And what, young lad, is so funny about that?'

'You...running...oh ha-ha...that's hilarious!'

'By running, I mean the running order by which we may be doing things.'

It's no use, the Boy Bing has tickled himself tremendously, and I'll just have to put up with his chuckles and sudden explosions of mirth. I wander into the lounge to deal with a marble mantlepiece clock, with a pretty chime.

I turn to find the lad, on the arm of a settee so as to gain sufficient height to watch my efforts.

The Ruminations of Bing

'So, guv, that grandfather clock in the study is the oldest ticker?'

'Yes, I should think so.'

I receive a mischievous look.

'You're a Grand pappy too, so I guess you and he were boys together, eh?'

'Bing, that ticker is nearly 200 years old!'

'So you were a teenager when he first appeared?'

Again, he dissolves into chuckles and hisses.

I have attempted on many an occasion to instruct Bing in basic history, and to give him an idea of the time-scale of events, but let's face it, if I get too involved, he merely shrugs and says...

'Hey I'm a hound. It's interesting, like a faint scent from over the fence, but I'm not going to fret over it.'

So that's me told.

Meanwhile, I have before me a small clock I found inside a box in the garage. With a certain amount of tinkering and much tup-tupping, I finally managed to get it going. Like

Tim Harnden-Taylor

many objects in our home, it has a mind of its own and sometimes when being wound, it decides to throw a fit and unwind its spring mighty speedily! At this point I threaten it by shouting "That's it, back in the box you go!" A short while later, I of course relent, and sit at the kitchen table fiddling and muttering until, once again, it ticks away merrily.

Clock duties over for another week, I'm now enjoying a particularly nice cup of coffee. A familiar hooter appears above the table top...

'Have we forgotten anything, guv?'

I peer over the top of my specs.

'No, I don't think so, clocks sorted, coffee made and toast on the go.'

'Being over 200 years old, guv, I understand your forgetfulness, but a certain chap has not had a treat.'

'Or three?'

'Quite, quite, old poop!'

The sun is shining, we decide to snack alfresco...we leave the house to our assorted 'tickers.'

Meanwhile...

Time marches on!

The Ruminations of Bing

Christmas

I rather like to think at this festive time, all around our jolly old globe, where Christmas celebrations take place, such scenes of affability are being shared. In this particular case, a certain hound (no names, no dog tags) and a suitably replete old poop are paying attention to a game of 'cracket' being beamed from the Antipodes, and more precisely, Melbourne.

One viewer (not me) is in his familiar upside down viewing position, gives a sniff as yet another batsman plays all around a ball and watches his 'castle' obey the laws of gravity, and tumble on to the 'track'.

'Coo, that was all rather odd, guv.'

'Yes, well, there are times when I wonder if watching such events is good for one's desire to remain merry and such.'

'Times, old poop?'

I look at my viewing pal, and wonder if he's bothered by the fall of another English wicket, or whether nationality is but the making of man? I decide now is not the time for such a chat. Crumbs, the prospect of 'Brexit' may even raise its 'ghostly' head!

'By *times*, Bing, I mean the Ashes are at this very moment being neatly packed and made ready to pop in the post to the Aussies.'

The lad wrinkles his hooter of renown, and after a slight pause, rests his chin on the arm rest of the couch.

'These Ashes, guv, are they a special snack?'

'Fortunately, they are not, Bing.'

'So why the fuss?'

'Well, the Ashes are a trophy that passes between England and Australia when one or the other wins the test series.'

Again, I wait while this new fact is filed into the noble mind in the section marked 'NON SNACKS...AND SUCH'.

'Well, kindly old gent, on the subject of snacks...'

'Yes?'

'Speaking as a non-Auntipoodlian, this here chap could manage a snack or three.'

Wandering back from the kitchen with a coffee for me and a few snacks for Bing, I'm greeted with...

'I've given this lot a sniff and they are apparently not noshable.'

'Well, Biblically speaking, Bing, I think we are some way from edible Nativities.'

'If you say so, guv.'

'Oh, I do, I do, I do, I do...I do.'

Of course, folks, it has to be a special day when well-timed snacks are produced at such a moment, thus taking a certain inquiring lad's mind off matters of a seasonal and theological note.

The Ruminations of Bing

It has of course been said before, but let us remember at this time, and from this particular corner of Epping Forest...The Only Way is Ethics.

(And such.)

Tim Harnden-Taylor

A Christmas Carol?

'I have been giving this some thought, aged guv.'

The lad has been quiet for quite some time and noticing this, I've continued to puzzle over a sentence that's failed to scan, from a new song.

'What's that, old fruit?'

'I was saying, ancient relic, I think I've worked out the answer to a bit of a poser.'

'Ancient relic? Ancient relic?'

'Yes, guv?'

'You're calling me an ancient relic?'

'If the beret fits, pop it on yer napper and wear it with pride...and so forth.'

Frankly I have no idea where Bingo gets these *'endearments'* from. Still, he gives me a winsome smile and I choose not to pursue the subject.

'The thing is, I've given this particular thought some real...um...er...'

'Thought?'

'Definitely, guv, and it occurs to me, we should settle down and write a suitably apt tara-diddle for the coming season.'

'I see.'

'Well, I reckon as a hound, I could come up with a few choice verses that will cheer the winter season, and possibly bring a tear to the eye.'

'A tear to the eye sounds about right, Bing.'

He fails to hear the irony in my voice and presses on.

'Got a bit of paper handy, guv?'

The Ruminations of Bing

I grab the trusty A4 pad, a pencil and, secretary like, await the pearls from the 'bard'.

'Now, let me see...

*'If...you...don't behave'ee,
You won't get gravy
On your Christmas pud! (Ruff – bark - woof!)
'If...you...don't cut the mustard
You'll get no custard
On your Christmas pud! (Growl – wiffle – huff!)
Your ears will sag,
And your tail won't wag
There'll be no such treats for you-oo
If you misbehaves, on Christmas days
And so forth and such this yeeeear!'*

The room falls silent, and I'm left wondering if the world is ready for this - yet.

Bing settles back on a couch and awaits my judgement.

'Well, um...it's...er...different?'

'It is, guv, yes, that's it, there is no doubt about it, it's different. *AND,* dare I say, a cut above "doggies in the window, woof-woof", and so forth.'

'Quite, quite.'

Tim Harnden-Taylor

His chin rests on the arm of the couch, and air of nonchalance upon his brow.

'I think if you give it a suitably interesting intro, followed by a bit of vamping...'

(Here I should point out that the lad had recently been listening to *Sinatra, Live at the Sands*.)

I start vamping on the piano...

He's off the couch and wagging his tail.

'Hello, LOWTOWN!...

> 'If...you...don't behave'ee,
> You won't get gravy
> On your Christmas pud! (Ruff – bark - woof!)
> 'If...you... don't cut the mustard
> You'll get no custard
> On your Christmas pud! (Growl – wiffle – huff!)
> Your ears will sag,
> And your tail won't wag
> There'll be no such treats for you-oo
> If you misbehaves, on Christmas days
> and so forth and such this yeeeear!'

The lad exits stage right...

Frankly folks...what more can be said?

(And this is only the beginning of Advent!!!!)

The Ruminations of Bing

Just One More Stroll...

How delicate the light seems, as it caresses the edge of each leaf on this small beech tree. It has sited itself between three mature guardians, and for the present, is quietly growing, part of the next generation of this ancient forest. Unaware of mortality, it's developing in its own time.

A sigh is heard and I realise it's me.

I turn my attention to a nearby holly bush, and the chap sniffing around the lower branches and a large tree stump beyond. My companion is totally at one with his environment. No complicated thoughts of future, no sentimentality towards the past, sure, this is what it's all about.

I look up, staring at a clear blue sky with a single vapour trail. The plane producing this is southward bound, and suddenly, there's a flash as the sun catches the angle between fuselage and wing and the course alters perceptibly.

Spring is young, and slowly with each day, it is rebuilding the canopy, as small buds are forming on the many trees. Soon we will hear them rustle in the wind and enjoy the shade they will give in the months ahead.

A paw is gently placed on my left knee, and I'm gazing at an expectant pal.

Tim Harnden-Taylor

'Can I help you, Bing?'

'A snack would be good, guv.'

The lad carefully relieves me of a snack or three, and I'm wondering if we might turn towards home.

'Guv?'

'M'mmmm?'

'I think I will never tire of this place.'

'Crumbs, Bing, that's a bit deep.'

The Ruminations of Bing

'Well, it's like this, old codger. When I'm having forty wags, I nearly always seem to venture here, and I feel very happy, even when I'm having to tow an old poop behind me!'

'Ah, yes, well, I guess that would be me...eh?'

'Nobody slower, guv.'

This ageing business is at times rather tough, but it's good to know the Boy Bing has been patient, and allowed me to trundle in his wake, around these paths. I like to think that even an eager hound is able to slow up a bit...and enjoy these small pleasures, in the company of an old wheeze box like me!

Our walk down the hill and home is bathed in sunlight. It warms our souls and creates delighted smiles upon hound and companion.

'Keep up, guv, we're nearly there!'

'We are indeed, Bing.'

Suddenly I feel rather sad, these little strolls will of course end...

...but perhaps not just yet.

Tim Harnden-Taylor

April Blooming Showers... and Such!

A huge droplet has trickled down the bridge of my nose, and having briefly hung from the end of it, decides to obey gravity and join the rest of the rain on the forest path.

'Sniff!'

Fellow droplets are now trundling around the rim of my ears, and forming earrings on the ends of my lobes, before copying the early nose drop!

'Sniff!'

Longish lengths of woodland grass are bowing under the weight of large raindrops...others of which are 'falling on my head!'

'Sniff, br'rrr, snuffle and sniff!'

Naturally my companion on this 'delightful' stroll is some yards ahead, happily sniffing the pathway and *hootering* the air, rather like some canine radar scanner.

The Ruminations of Bing

'Isn't it luvverly, guv?'

Before answering, I'm recalling the time; not twenty minutes before, when we'd strolled out into a pleasantly warm morning, and I panted my way up the path, being led by a beaming Bing, and entered our dear old forest. Now, I'm slithering and sliding down a muddy path, trying to gather my thoughts before proffering the lad a reply!

'I was saying, guv...'

A scent is received into the hooter, and I perceive that he's rummaging around his vast mental lexicon of memorable 'pongs'.

'M'mmm, crocus, I reckon. Yes, as I was saying, old poop, isn't it simply heavenly out here today.'

Careful, H-T, choose your words carefully. Remember the Boy Bing is built for such perambulations. He cannot understand your desire to find a suitable place where the only water is contained within a glass of hops!

I'm assuming that the lad's remark is purely rhetorical, as I receive a grin and he trundles on towards a pond.

Tim Harnden-Taylor

The expression 'it's too wet for ducks' comes to mind, for, as we stand on a stage, the feathered inhabitants are not to be seen. Not for them a rain drenching, they are far too sensible. No, they are snugly ensconced in their thatched reed homes! Well, if they have any sense, they are!

'M'mm, that's odd, guv, not a sign of 'em'.

'Well, Bing...'

My voice trails away as three moorhens decide to appear and, 'Wilson, Keppel & Betty' like, nod and bob their way across the water before disappearing under a low bridge.

'Sniff.'

'There you are, guv, I knew we'd see some folk down here.'

The enthusiasm of my companion is really a wonder, for here I am, trying to ignore the assault from more huge rain drops, feeling decidedly damp...and yet...and yet I'm smiling like a simpleton.

The sun decides to peep through.

The Ruminations of Bing

'Sniff!!!!'

Am I dreaming? Is Bing humming *The Sun has Got His Hat On*? I know he's heard me hum it a few times but can it be true? Frankly, when it comes to the Boy Bing, nothing surprises me.

Tim Harnden-Taylor

Spotting The Eyes and Crossing The Teas

There are days when finally, my conscience gets the better of me and I decide it's time for another session of tidying 'the study'.

Naturally, the most uncluttered person I know is a certain hound, sun-basking in the hallway just outside the study. I've glanced at him several times over the course of the last hour or so, and he's barely changed position. Occasionally his hooter of renown has crinkled and snorted, and front paws have chivvied the carpet in an attempt to scrape a dreamed 'goodie' off a path. Even his back legs have made the odd kick and bounding action. Clearly by this observation, you can tell how easily I am distracted.

I am old enough to remember a wireless programme from way back when, called *Music While You Work*. Since its demise, I have kept up the tradition of playing music as I busy myself, particularly in 'the study'. I should, for the sake of fairness, point out that I think it's all right to call this particular room by this name, (grand as it might sound), as it is here I attempt to lick the *Tales of Bing* and this aged poop into a form of English, that just about passes muster...and such.

The longer these 'moments' go on, the more I feel like John Watson, bringing readers up to date with the latest marvels of Sherlock Holmes. I might go as far as suggesting I could be Dr Johnson's ever faithful Boswell. However, as the only thing that would pass for Scotch coursing through my veins is of the bottled variety, I fear I'd better drop that thought and continue with this particular morning.

Music is playing as I attempt to work!

The Ruminations of Bing

My morning started with an old 'live' recording of Thomas Beecham conducting the Sibelius *2nd Symphony* and that having come to a 'Finnish', I've trundled off elsewhere. Now, as I cram more unwanted paper into the 'strimmer', as Bing calls it, I'm foot-tapping and smiling along with the mighty Jack Teagarden and Bobby Hackett. Quite what Beecham or Sibelius would make of this, I cannot tell, but as they won't be popping into 'Lyons' this particular morning, I'll risk their glowering.

Talking of popping in, I'm suddenly aware of a noble brow observing me. A throat is cleared.

'I have made every effort, guv, to remain uninterested in your latest 'strimming' attempts, but frankly, it has to be said that your choices of music along with 'buzz-saw' solos are not conducive to a bit of mid-morning shuteye and so forth.'

'Ah.'

'Ah, indeed, old poop.'

'Could I suggest a snack might cool your ardent brow?'

'Well, the prospect of 'chomping' on two to three such chaps might cure any possible agitation.'

We trundle to the kitchen and the snack tin acts as our mediator to any possible awkwardness.

The morning, and therefore the day, looks mighty fine and a turn around the back garden with a mug of tea for fuel is just the thing.

It has to be said that I'm really not much of a gardener, although I do get a certain relaxation from deadheading plants and shrubs as required. Even old duffers can spot when a flower is no longer a going concern. I've watched happily as Monty Don has busied himself in his rather fine garden, along with his two retriever helpers. Of course, I'm rather daunted by the number of jobs he tackles AND the fact that, when it comes to popping a plant, shrub, tree or such in the ground, the soil positively parts like the proverbial Red Sea. Meanwhile, the typical London clay at 'Lyons' can defeat both pick axe and, dare I say, diamond tipped drill. That is why we have most of our plants in tubs and pots and such...sorry about that, Monty.

Bing has been wandering around and become quite engrossed in a corner patch that once, I feel, was the haunt of a lilac, now it appears to have morphed into privet. I offer no other observation to this matter other than once where there was lilac, there's now privet. Meanwhile...very slowly, Bing is extricating himself, by means of reverse gear, from the depths of privet and, on turning, has clamped in his mouth an extremely ancient-looking tennis ball. He drops it at my feet.

'Go on, give it a chuck, you know you want to.'

Mustering a look of enthusiasm, I pick up the grotty damp pill, and sling it across the lawn.

The lad turns and fairly flashes across the grass, and soon

The Ruminations of Bing

returns with it. However, he wanders to a sunny patch and carefully places his new-found pal dead centre.

'I think it could do with a good drying out, guv.'

'Well, it did appear a trifle damp.'

'So would you be, guv, if you lived under that there hedge in all weathers.'

'M'mmmm.'

I notice a robin inspecting the ball. He is not impressed and bounces off to settle on the lip of a pot containing lemon-smelling mint. Bing is back in the thick of the privet, and there I shall leave him for the moment as Mr Teagarden and Mr Hackett are awaiting my return to foot-tapping duties.

Tim Harnden-Taylor

Seeing and Getting the Point

We were just about to cross a bridle path and start our stroll home the other day, when the Boy Bing suddenly sat and looked left with such an eager look that I decided I'd better stop and see what his sudden halt was all about.

Seconds later, a horse with rider came trotting along the path and halted a few feet from us. The lad had a quiet chat with the steed, and I made an unremarkable observation about the weather to the horsewoman. She politely agreed with me about the possibility of a shower later, and yes, wasn't this Saharan dust a nuisance?

Having exhausted our repertoire of small talk, I was delighted to observe that the horse/dog chat had reached a conclusion and moments later, horse and rider clip-clopped off in the opposite direction of our meander.

Shortly after, as we paused for snacks and such, my wandering mind was brought up short as the lad proffered the following.

'Well, old poop, that was all very interesting.'

'It was your usual snack or three, Bing.'

The Ruminations of Bing

'No, guv, not that, you silly, I was making reference to my recent chat with Ralph.'

'Ralph?'

'Certainly, guv, certainly. The horse.'

'Ah.'

'Ah, indeed, old fruit. I asked him if he was one of the chaps we saw bounding over the fences at the Grand National.'

'I see.'

'Well, old poop, it appears he wasn't and only partakes in point to points and such like.'

'And so forth, Bing.'

'Very likely, guv.'

I sat for a few seconds, absorbing this information.

'Guv?'

'Yes, m'boy?'

'Dare I ask you what a point to point is? Or would it be pointless to ask you to point out the relevance of point to point and its meaning?'

'Well...'

'I mean, guv, if you're not sure, I guess we can noodle it when we get home.'

'Noodle...?'

'Yes, guv.'

'M'mmmm...oh, you mean Google!'

'Very likely, old poop.'

'Well, Bing, in this case, I do happen to understand the meaning of point to point.'

'Hurrah!'

Tim Harnden-Taylor

'It's the name given to races which trundle from one point to another.'

'Well, I never did.'

'Quite, Bing, you never did.'

Figuring that I'd just about exhausted my knowledge of point to points and so forth, I thought it an ideal moment for us to trundle on our way.

Down the passage that leads home we go, hopefully today there will be no discarded takeaways or 'hissy' cats to slow our progress. In the distance, we can hear the children out in the school playground and a bell sounds to call them to order.

Our gentle stroll is coming to an end, the lad has inspected a large pot of lavender positively glowing in the shade of a driveway. Little things, great pleasures, and I know my companion feels very much the same way. Let's face it, it's old poops like me who complicate things...and such.

The Ruminations of Bing

Spring?

We have wandered along a new path this morning. For some reason, I have been happy to let the lad trundle along various trails, and I believe I have a reasonable idea of roughly where we are. It's actually a sunny day, so I guess we should make the most of this unexpected bonus.

Bing is impervious to what the elements can chuck at us, so my pleasure is slightly different to his.

'You okay, old huff and puff?'

I try not to sound too puffed as I reply, 'Certainly, Bing, certainly.'

I get a couple of wags from the tail just in front and we plough on down through a path skirted by ferns, little holly bushes, and fallen tree trunks coated with various fungi. Once again, I wish I knew which ones of these would be mighty tasty if popped into a pan. Back in the 'Land of his Fathers', such a hound as Bing might well be used for truffle hunting, but this particular offshoot from the Vendée area of France seems more inclined to worry with his hooter at my jacket pockets when it comes to nosh!

A small pond is ahead and I realise it's not one we have ventured to before but am delighted to realise that if we trundle up a nearby slope, my panting will be rewarded by a mighty fine pub that resides beside the forest!

Tim Harnden-Taylor

'Um, Bing, shall we go that way?'

'What? Up to the boozer at the top?'

'H-h-h-ow did you know????'

'Guv, you and I have certain trundles we like.'

'Yes?'

'Tom and I often come this way, and, guv, you'll find it hard to believe, we nearly always end up at The Foresters.'

'The Foresters?'

'Certainly, guv, certainly.'

Yet again the lad amazes me with his 'local' knowledge, and the thought of this particular 'local' gives me added impetus, and I puff and pant up the slope, with my 'sherpa' kindly giving me a tow!

As we reach the edge of the forest, the sky is looking particularly threatening, and so the inner confines are reached quickly and whilst the lad has a mighty drink of water, I have water as well…in the shape of a foaming pint of water with the finest Kentish hops!

'Cor, that's better, guv, eh?'

'It certainly is, young lad.'

'Got a…?'

'Treat or three?'

'Cough 'em up, guv, and I'll make sure I get you home without getting lost!'

'Bing, I happen to know this old forest like the back of my …'

'Head, guv?'

'I was going to say, back of my hand.'

'Which one?'

The Ruminations of Bing

'Um...'

'Enough said, guv.'

Give up, H-T, you know you're on a loser.

'How's your pint, guv?'

'Oh, I'm very "hoppy" with it, ha-ha!'

Bing exchanges a look with a nearby whippet, who looks far too snooty for my liking.

Later, as we trundle downhill through old Lowtown...

'Darlene thought you were a simpleton, guv.'

'Darlene?'

'Yes, guv, you know, the flounce with the bounce.'

'Oh, the whippet.'

'That's the one.'

'Why would she think that?'

Tim Harnden-Taylor

'Because I told her you were.'

'Charming.'

'Yes, that's it, guv, a charming old simpleton.'

'Best get me home before I forget where the snack tin resides.'

I receive a frown from the hound of renown.

'Not funny, guv, not funny at all.'

The Ruminations of Bing

Orchestrated Manoeuvres in the Bark

Being the sort of trundler I am, you, the observer of my days spent with a certain hound, presently sitting a few feet from me as I rattle the old qwerty, will be aware the lad uses the gift of his low growl, woof and Baskerville howl, sparingly.

Not for him the chitter-chatter of *some* very bossy terriers, or uncontrollable *chuntering* of certain *'growlers'* who continue to stress long after their point is made. (A frightful vision of Prime Minister's *Question Time* from the Hounds of Parliament just wafted into mind.)

No, Bing is not afflicted with any of the above, and any other forms of excitability...and such.

Frankly, a well-timed 'woof!' will generally bring matters back under control, as many a bossy magpie, crow and so forth can and should jolly well attest.

(pause)

Now, where was I? (I just had to provide a snack or three for the lad. Well, he's such a polite chap, and really, it was no bother pausing momentarily.)

Oh, yes, we were chatting about over-aggressiveness. It brings to mind an instance a few days ago when...

'So sorry to interrupt your flow, guv, but I was just wondering if you had seen the main controller?'

'Do you mean Alison?'

'Oh, you're such a card, old fluffy bonce.'

'Fluffy bonce?'

'Certainly, guv, certainly.'

'Are you referring to my newly washed hair, which does

become *fly away* when washed?'

'Where to?'

'Where to, Bing?'

'Yup. It looks as if it's getting ready to fly off, and it'll be great as I've often wondered what a bald old coot looks like.'

'Really?'

'Honestly, guv, you must be the easiest person to baffle.'

'M'mmmm.'

'Talking of tea, any chance of you topping up my water bowl?'

(pause)

Now, where was I?

Oh, yes, when it comes to dealing with houseguests, it's nice to think one can facilitate any special needs, thus keeping an all round laid back atmosphere to the fore. Why, only the other day, we had family popping in from New Zealand. Fortunately, they're extremely easygoing or maybe just very polite. Well, Bing, of course, was in his element, making them feel at home by kindly offering them use of any number of his telly-viewing couches.

'Now there's a real darling, guv.'

'M'mmm?'

'Emma.'

'Oh, yes.'

'Let's face it, old noggin', it couldn't possibly be you, eh?'

'Yes, she takes after her mother, don't y'know?'

'Quite.'

The Ruminations of Bing

'It was a real treat to see them. They live on the other side of the world.'

'Coo, near Chingford?'

Make a note, H-T, to attempt, once again, the near impossible conception that an enormous amount of what we folk call 'The World' exists beyond the outer regions of Bing's hooter!

Nevertheless...

(pause)

Finally, the main TV controller has been unearthed, the boy is now happily settled in front of today's stage of the Tour de France, with a couple of snacks awaiting the next feeding stage prior to the Pyrenees.

Now, where was I? Today seems full of um...er...

'Interruptions, guv?'

'Quite.'

Tim Harnden-Taylor

Henrys and Georges and Such

After a rather pleasing lunch, I adjourned to the lounge, and having settled down to a documentary regarding Henry II, it wasn't long before Morpheus gently settled on my brow and Henry's problems with Thomas Becket faded as I opted to rest my eyes.

Time trundled by and I became aware of the clearing of a throat. I raised one eyelid and focused in the direction of the throat clearer. Of course it's Bing, sitting as ever very neatly, head slightly cocked and ears pricked ready to receive any information.

Slowly I raised my other eyelid and cleared my throat.

'Ah, hello, Bing, have you been there long?'

'If by *long*, guv, you mean, did I hear your hooter buzzing like a swarm of bees collecting honey? Then I most certainly have.'

'I see.'

'Well, you do now, guv, now you've opened up for business once again.'

'I was merely resting my eyes, all the better to take in the historical facts regarding Henry the Second.'

The Ruminations of Bing

'So, what did he come second in, guv?'

'Who?'

'Henry.'

'Ah, actually he was the second Henry.'

'I see. So, who was first?'

'Um, er... well, Henry the First.'

'First of what?'

'Well, England, of course.'

'So who came after the second Henry?'

'Bing, I fear this is getting rather complicated. You see when I say Henry the Second came after Henry the First, I was merely putting him in the order of kings named Henry, and not in their actual order as Kings of England...and such.'

'So it was not a race in which Henry came Second after the Henry who won?'

'Correct.'

'Cor, you two legged folk don't half know how to confuse a chap.'

'Well, the thing is, Bing, the Kings and Queens of this sceptred isle stretch back over a very long time.'

'I see.'

'Jolly good.'

'When I say, I see, what I really mean is... I haven't a clue what you're talking about.'

It was now time for me to say...'I see.'

'For instance, guv, how many kings called Henry have there been?'

'Eight, so far.'

Tim Harnden-Taylor

'M'mmmm.' The lad is attempting to compute this.

'Also, there have been four Williams, three Richards, eight Edwards, six Georges, a John, one Stephen. I haven't mentioned the Queens yet and also there were many kings before William the First, who beat Harold in 1066 and all that!'

'Guv.'

'Yes, Bing?'

'I think you'd better stop as you lost me shortly after this septic isle...and such.'

'Ah.'

'Being a sporting sort of chap, I got rather excited when you mentioned Henry coming second. I thought I had discovered a new sporting event.'

'You mean the original *Game of Thrones?*'

'Guv, I really haven't a clue why you should find that so funny.'

'Oh, ha, ha, ha, he,he,he!'

Exit Bing.

It is while I'm gathering myself after my sudden burst of laughter, albeit to a totally mystified Bing, I hear...

'If it's not too much to ask, there's a chap out here sitting in front of a certain well known snack tin, and wondering if there's a chance of a munch or three?'

Enough said.

The Ruminations of Bing

Brexits and Exits

As you know, Bing is usually of a very sunny disposition. I write this because, on this particular morning when the lad arrived, he trundled past me with barely a nod and, having accepted his usual two-snack starter, wandered out into the garden and sat staring at the builders currently extending the house over the road.

Time with Bing has taught me to continue with my day as if all is well, and wait for the boy to trundle up and enlighten me regarding his current frown.

I took a mug of tea and one of the current books I'm reading into the garden and settled down for a good read. Well, I attempted to, but was soon aware of a pair of very keen eyes looking at me from time to time.

A throat cleared, it wasn't mine.

'Frankly, ol' wrinkly chops, after all our time spent together, I thought you could at least be relied upon to keep a chap up to date with matters of such importance.'

'What? The house extension over the way?'

Tim Harnden-Taylor

'Don't be silly, guv, I'm well up with most of the building projects going on around this 'ere neck of the woods.'

Where the lad gets such expressions from never ceases to amaze and baffle me. (Yes, I realise I'm not the sharpest knife in the drawer, thank you very much!)

'Hello, his mind's gone for a wander. Oi!'

My mind bumped back into the present.

The lad settles very neatly in front of me and peers into my eyes, as if determining whether there's a light on in the old chump's attic space! The clearing of the throat leads me to believe he has deemed me worthy of an attempt.

'What it is, old chump, is that I'm been continually buffeted by talk of a "BREXIT!" '

Not only was my mind back in the present, I felt myself fluttering skyward and preparing to go into such a tailspin of extreme dizziness that, for a moment, I understood how poor old Icarus must have felt! I had, I thought, completely managed to avoid all mention of the dreaded 'B' word.

A throat was cleared, this time my own.

'Ah, well, yes, you see, um, what is it that you are concerned about?'

'The whole caboodle and so forth.'

'Well, Bing...'

'I mean, guv, most important of all is the matter of a hard or soft BREXIT.'

'Quite, Bing...yes, quite...er...quite.'

'Is that it, old fount of knowledge and suchlike?'

I stared into my empty mug and the remnants of a dunked digestive, and realised it would be like dredging the mouth of the Humber, if I was determined to quaff the remains.

My mine blazed into action.

The Ruminations of Bing

'The thing is, my lad...'

'Need another cuppa?'

I grasped at this lifeline and tried to appear unconcerned about the matter of Brexit. I almost looked in control.

'Back in a tick, Bing.'

'I await the words of wisdom with great alacrity, guv.'

I nearly blurted out 'cripes' but fortunately a fit of coughing overtook me. Yes, I'd decided to tackle the bottom of the tea mug in what I thought would be a nonchalant manner. Will I never learn?

I refreshed the old beaker and peered into the garden. Drat, the lad was sitting very neatly next to my garden chair. I grabbed a snack or three from the tin, and trundled out, hoping the lad would become absorbed with tackling the goodies and therefore forget the dreaded Brexit!

Oh, I know...some chance of that.

I'm sure I will have mentioned at sometime or such, that all the other pals who've spent time in the 'Lyons' set up, have all been what I would term guzzle merchants, when it came to the matter of nosh in all its various forms. Bing is much more your gastronome, and whereas he can become fixated by the various scents emanating from just about everywhere, his intake is what I would deem fussy. In short, he really has no idea just how amazed we are with his decidedly individualistic palate.

I received a nudge from a certain chap's 'hooter'.

Snacks were carefully received and placed neatly before him. He would not be distracted from...

'Brexit, guv, B-R-E-X-I-T!!'

The two builders working from the scaffolding over the road decided to take a break and both leaned in my direction. I believe they had been listening in all along.

Tim Harnden-Taylor

Not for the first time this particular morning, I cleared my throat...

'Now, Bing, when it comes to the matter of Brexit and whether one should opt for a hard or soft one...'

'Ye-e-e-sss?'

'Ultimately it comes down to one's own matter of, um...er ...taste.'

'That's fair enough, guv. I mean, I don't like anything too crunchy, but there again, tooooo soft and there is a certain lack of satisfaction on the palate.'

'Quite, quite, Bing. I do believe you have summed up the whole conundrum beautifully.'

'In short and such, guv, what you are telling me is that folk can't agree on the sort of palatability of these 'ere Brexits?'

'I certainly believe we have arrived at the nub of this particular dilemma.'

'I hope you won't be too offended if I proffer the following thought on this extraordinary Brexit business, old poop?'

'Feel free, dear lad.'

The Ruminations of Bing

'Guv, you two-legged trundlers seem to be rather proficient at complicating matters.'

'I see.'

'Let's face it, when it comes to complicating matters, and dare I add, sullying the bottom of your tea mugs and suchlike, you lot are frankly a right shower.'

'I see.'

'It's all a matter of timing, do you see.'

'Um...' (Surely I could have done better than that?)

'Concentrate on the matter at hand, guv, don't let your minds wander. If dunking is your thing, then treat it with respect. Don't, and I can't emphasise this enough, just plunge yer Brexit in your mug and forget the metamorphosis that instantly takes place on entry to the hot liquid.'

Don't say it, H-T...

'I see.' (Damn!)

'This way, one can achieve the ultimate delight, without creating a mush in yer mug.'

At this point, the lad picked up one of his treats, and as gently as ever, gave it all his attention.

Meanwhile, an old codger breathed a sigh of relief, and yet couldn't help thinking the matter of Brexit might well raise its head again above the parapet of 'The Corner House' sometime in the near future.

Over the road, the two leaning builders had decided to indulge in a spot of pebble-dashing, and I discovered I'd brought the wrong book out to read!

Tim Harnden-Taylor

Arthurian Legends...

Somewhere in the Wood of Brent
An Arthur and a Bing did went
On the trail the two did go
For to hunt the Gruffalo.

How high and wide is a Gruffalo
And will he smile and say hello?

Could he fit inside this crack?

The Ruminations of Bing

Oh no, I think I've found a track.

'I do believe he went that-a-way...'

And Bing said, 'We'll go the other way.'

Tim Harnden-Taylor

'Don't worry Bing, he's not that gruff
And you well know you're rough and tuff...'

'Well, that didn't take too long to find...
Did we leave our Bing behind?'

The Ruminations of Bing

He found the scent of something else,
Of scones and jam and pots of cream...
For 'tis of such delightful things

... that our Boy Bing would like to dream.

Tim Harnden-Taylor

The Rain Has Stopped... For The Moment!

My companion this morning is taking the air in the garden. I find his keen interest in 'patrolling' this area really interesting. He is, of course, quite unaware of me and is slowly manoeuvring his hooter gently towards a plant that is obviously giving off a tremendous scent.

He suddenly pulls his head back, wrinkles his nose and watches a large bumblebee drone away to another flower.

'Crumbs, guv, that was a bigg'un!'

He looks over at me, and I try to look as if his sudden comment has made me look up from the paper I've been pretending to read.

'I find them such amiable chaps, Bing.'

'Really?'

'Oh, yes.'

'Give me a f'rinstance, guv.'

'Well...um...ah, yes, well, if one of those chaps should venture into the house, it is quite easy to show them the way out.'

The Ruminations of Bing

'Not like Stingy-wapsits and Whizzers eh?'

'Quite...quite.'

Off goes Bing on another circuit, and I decide another cup of coffee would be rather nice.

As I wait for the kettle to boil, I can see the lad has found a warm patch of grass in the sun and is currently having a gentle roll before taking a quick snooze, or 'forty wags', as he calls it. Meanwhile, I'm delighted to roust out a Kit Kat and, mug in hand, return to my seat. The lad is dozing. There follows the quietest rip of confectionery wrapper and instantly Bing is alert and at my side.

'Hello, hello, hello...having a snack, old guv?'

'Well, just a...'

'Anything for a real pal and decent egg, if ever there was one?'

'Possibly.' A Bing-type snack is proffered and gently accepted.

'I suppose you'll be hoovering the grass soon?'

'Well, I guess it would be a good idea to get the old Flymo out and have a quick session.'

Tim Harnden-Taylor

'Well, let me know when, and I'll go in and see if there's any twenty-twenty 'crackit' on the box.'

Bing is not a fan of Flymos or Henrys.

'Right-ho, Bing.'

For the moment, though, we'll just take it easy and savour the warmth of this lovely morning.

My companion has found a fresh area of warm grass... rolling has recommenced.

On the whole, taking everything into account, by and large, and so forth and...

'Suchlike, guv?'

'Certainly, Bing, certainly.'

It's been a kind, and in this corner of Lowtown, generous summer morning.

The Ruminations of Bing

Life From 1 - 6....And So Forth

Man (and by that, I mean woman as well) is a complex being. Trying to fathom their likes and also dislikes can be quite a performance and, on occasion, can disappoint or please one. (One being me...or you, if you see what I mean.) In short, despite my age and therefore assumed experience of life, dealing with my fellow 'man' can at times lead to unexpected complications.

On the other hand...

Dogs (and by this, I'm thinking of a particular visitor to this homestead) are, by and large, taking all in all and so forth and suchlike, a much less complicated kettle of fish... or should that be kennel of dogs?

When it comes to passing an uncomplicated time with such pals, it's very much less of a strain. (Generally.)

For our canine pals, life is very much more, um...well...less difficult. They may seem to be a trial at times, but most of their day is spent dealing with the premise...

1: Is it edible?

2: If not, move on.

Tim Harnden-Taylor

Fellow idlers who've cast their eyes over these jottings will have noticed that the 'lad' differs from many of his fellow barkers and woofers. Once one understands that he is a 'talker', the other most extraordinary difference is his fussiness when it comes to 'nosh'.

All the other 'tail waggers' we've entertained over the years have had healthy appetites and thus have happily 'chomped' their way through wide ranging varieties of grub. (Both authorised and unauthorised.)

With Bing we get...

1: Is it edible?

2: Do my taste buds find this item toothsome?

3: Might I prefer to tackle this a little later?

4: Is that elderly gent (me) eyeing it up?

5: A hiding place is required.

6: Move on.

Is it not enough that this hound looks upon me as an old huff and puff, and continually refers to me as 'aged' or 'old wrinkly chops' and other such 'delightful' epithets?

Goodness knows I've tried most particularly over the years to guide his questing 'hooter' for knowledge, in a way that could advance his education.

The Ruminations of Bing

Despite my best endeavours, his view of life seems a tad askew...or is it?

I ask this because today, conversation passed between us that, once again, throws my entire belief in being 'the master' into a thorough tailspin, leaving me not only puzzled but rather wobbly on m'old pins!

We had, as is our Friday wont, settled down to a quiet session of Australian Rules football, with Bing thoroughly interested in the gent that trundles between the posts and gestures most emphatically as to the type of score that's been made.

He truly believes it's the same person at both ends of the pitch, who somehow manages to scuttle between ends at a rate of knots, always able to anticipate which side will score next.

It's not for the likes of an old poop to tell him the truth, and so I happily let him 'wonder' at the speed of certain antipodean referees. Frankly, I think it wise to allow certain 'mysteries' to be maintained, even if it means I 'up' gents from Down Under, who, I dare say, *don't* deserve it!

It was while a member of one of the teams was being treated for a nasty tumble, with the time-honoured sponge of cold water, that I noticed Bing rummaging around on the couch, and on the point of totally dismantling the cushions thereon!

Tim Harnden-Taylor

'Bing!'

My companion paused in his efforts and threw a 'Yes, guv?' over his shoulder before continuing.

'Bing, what are you trying to do?'

'You know my 1, 2, 3, 4, 5, 6, guv?' (See rules above.)

'Yes, I am conversant with your rules regarding possible *'nosh'*, Bing.'

'Well, I do believe I shall have to add a 7th.'

'Really, Bing?'

'Certainly, guv, certainly.'

'The seventh being?'

'If at first you do not chew, dive and try again.'

Finally a small piece of 'buried' Bonio was discovered, and the lad settled once more to the *'trundlers'* on screen.

'One other thing, guv.'

'Not an *8th* surely?'

'Don't be silly, old poop...'

'Well?'

'When's the snooker on?'

The Ruminations of Bing

'Soon, Bing, very soon...'
'Just time for a snack or three?'
'Well...'
'Jolly good...I'm starving.'
'M'mmmm.'

Tim Harnden-Taylor

And For Those Of You Watching In Black & White

'Wotcha!'

The familiar cheeky look of a certain hound is peering at me as I busy myself with study tidying.

'Ah, Bing m'boy, how you going?'

'On four paws as usual, guv.'

His long hooter twitches, eyebrows are raised...I await the next lines with keen interest.

A throat is cleared.

'I was just wondering, ol' chubby chops, if there was any possibility of a certain aged poop wandering through to the finest room of the house' (the kitchen) 'and possibly, coughing up a couple of snacks for this 'ere chap?'

'Well...'

The Ruminations of Bing

A chin is rested on my knee, brown eyes flutter in my direction.

'I guess I could stop for a...'

'Good, good...orf we jolly well go.'

The confidence that exudes from this chap is quite ridiculous. Why he should think I am here merely to pander to his needs is quite ridiculous.

However, I arrive in the kitchen to find the boy seated very neatly next to the snack shelf.

Grub is received and the lad trundles off into the garden.

At this point, coffee is poured and, seated at the kitchen table, I look out at the garden beyond and the lad who's 'beating the bounds' thereof.

Thus, as the Bard would have it, the 'daily round' is underway. Outside, the day is very blustery, and frankly not the weather for an old poop to venture out in. Unlike the Boy Bing, I am not impervious to 'weather'. I look to warmer days hence, when once again, both of us can enjoy a stroll down the familiar paths we both love.

I receive a nudge from a hooter to my knee.

'Knowing what a sporting 'toff' you are, guv, I thought you'd like to know the snooker's back on the box.'

'Is it, Bing?'

'Yep, and if you get a hurry on, you might get the comfy seat!'

'Really?'

'Nope, but I like to see you trundle at speed!'

(Trundling at speed is attempted...I come a tardy second.)

The 'click' of snooker is underway, the lad is viewing at his usual 'snookering' angle. I, on the other hand, will be boring and not defy gravity.'

Tim Harnden-Taylor

'You sissy,' says Bing.

'M'mmm,' says I.

The Ruminations of Bing

'The thing is, old wrinkly chops...'

Bing and I are sitting in the garden, enjoying some unexpectedly warm days. I'm sipping a cuppa and the lad has returned to my side for snacks, having inspected the grounds and such.

'Yes, the thing is, old poop, I'm starting to feel a change in the air.'

'Ah, yes, Bing, the summer has given up on us and the next season is, as we chat, forming an orderly queue, champing at the bit to make its presence known.'

'Let's face it, old wobbly cheeks, the uncommonly warm weather we've had this 'ere summer has seriously restricted your observations regarding the weather and whether such weather is worth weathering or whether it...er...'

'Isn't?'

'Quite, quite.'

'Well, Bing, I'm sorry if my conversation might occasionally centre around the meteorological conundrums, which, living in jolly old Lowtown, can dominate one's decision as to should one pop a sweater on or boldly venture out umbrella-less...and such.'

'Blimey, what an adventurous chap you are, guv.'

'Do I detect a hint of cynicism in your voice, Bing?'

'Coo, that isn't a hint you're detecting, guv, it's a dirty great dollop of it with Christmas lights and tambourine ensemble tippy-tapping on your bonce.'

'Charming.'

'I hope, oh mighty bumble-boots, I've managed to convey with due accuracy, the extreme need you have for all matters conversational, when it comes to any or all events pertaining to what you chaps call *weather*, and we hounds earnestly can find no importance.'

'M'mmm, Bing, you sound rather Wilde...ha-ha!'

'Once again, you've lost me, guv.'

'What? No Oscar?'

'I refer you to my previous statement.'

Being the sort of old poop I am, I'm rather pleased with having extricated myself from my usual losing position. It can't, and won't, last.

'Now, guv, while I have some semblance of your undivided attention, may I observe that you seem to have changed colour?'

'I must say, Bing, spending more time out in the garden weeding and so forth, I seem to have taken on a tan.'

'Good heavens, how could that happen?'

Not being the sharpest knife in the cutlery drawer, you will not be surprised by...

'Oh, it's the wonderful weathe-...'

'Ha! Ha! Got you!'

Beaten by a Hound! (Well, not just any hound.)

Obsession, of course, is in the eye or senses of the beholder. For me, apparently, it's the weather. For a certain chap sitting nearby, it's the rattle of the snack tin.

One rattle and some semblance of order is restored.

Well, sort of.

The Ruminations of Bing

The Art of Dozing

A low growl, a nozzle quiver and back foot 'Thumper' kick.

Bing is over for the day, and having exhausted himself with some snooker viewing, he is having a quick nap before the latest round of ski jumping.

Being the great observer I am, I'm...um...observing him in repose.

Here he is then, lying on his chosen settee, and out like the proverbial light!

Let's begin with his tail, which occasionally flicks, before breaking into a full wag. Next, the rear legs. Being the French hound he is, his 'kippers' are remarkably structured, with large paws designed to pad their way through the marshy region in the Vendée. Well, in truth, his ancestors came from there, he actually comes from the mysterious land of roundabouts, known as Milton Keynes.

Thus we reach his front paws. These suddenly appear to be doing a doggy paddle type action. It is, however, arriving at his noble brow, that we notice the wobble of eyebrows and furrowing of forehead. Naturally the 'hooter' is his most important organ, and it twitches in unison with oscillating nostrils as, within his dream, he searches the scent of greatest importance!

Here then is the lad dozing...

'WOOF!'

'Um...er...what...what? Oh, it's you, Bing.'

'It is indeed, oh, snoozing poop!'

'What, what?'

'Cor, I don't know, guv, you were miles away.'

'Ah, well, I was just, um, resting the old eyes...and such.'

'Resting? Resting? Guv, they were slammed shut!'

'I think you exaggerate.'

'Sorry, guv, but an old poop having a nap is quite sight to behold.'

'Really?'

'Certainly, gaffer, certainly.'

'M'mmm.'

'Your old plates jibber now and then, and you have a habit of drumming the armchair arms with your fingers, as if you're playing the piano or somesuch-thingy-wotsit.'

The Ruminations of Bing

'I see.'

'As for your old noddle? Well, I've never seen such activity. Your upper lip seems to buzz now and then, whilst your old hooter will suddenly snort as you awaken momentarily before recommencing your snooze.'

'Oh, Bing, I do believe you are, as usual, exaggerating.'

'Please yourself, guv, makes no odds to me.'

'M'mmmm.'

'All I can say, oh, great buddha of the armchair, is that you appear to be more active in your dreams than awake!'

'Charming.'

'Merely an observation, guv.'

'M'mmm.'

'Talking of m'mmm...how about a snack and such?'

'Well...'

'Come on, guv, stir your stumps, let's trundle off to the kitchen and stoke up, before those chaps start leaping off that slide.'

Tim Harnden-Taylor

Thoughts From France... But Of Home!

I'm pretty sure it would be no exaggeration, if I said the Boy Bing is a hound of extraordinary discernment. I speak as one who has, over the years, known many of our *'best friends'* and their ability to *'nosh'* just about anything that has come in close proximity to their 'chops'!

Where this lad is so different is in his apparently delicate palate. All his regular pals would not hesitate in agreeing.

We have all become aware of his talent for *not* just downing *'grub'* willy-nilly. No, here we appear to have a *bon viveur* of the first, and very likely second, water!

Before we attempt to elevate this chap to the 'foody' equivalent of beatification, I should point out that he has been known to 'lapse'. Such occasions occur when what appears to be an insignificant morsel is tackled with all the enthusiasm and gusto any one of us would show, when delighting in our own favourite comfort food!

The Ruminations of Bing

This said, he is not one to be led on by such comments as *'M'mmm, Bing, this is really lovely'* or *'This is so toothsome, I wouldn't mind it myself.'* He has such a way of peering at you, as if calling your bluff! He'll then shrug and turn away with never a backward glance. *IF* the proffered 'nosh' has an interesting 'pong', then the lad will gently relieve you of the tit-bit and wander off to a quiet spot for further investigations. However, it is not unusual to find this item parked in another place, having been abandoned as *'not required on board'*.

As I've said, it has been my observation, over the years, that such behaviour is contrary to the normal reactions of our family *'barkers'*. In short, I recall one black Labrador who delighted in unzipping used tea bags and then spitting the contents out with disgust, only to tackle a second, third and so on, in the belief that one day, one of these soggy sacks would contain the mother lode of doggy delights! Undimmed, dear old Bess tackled tea bags from puppy to grey-chops!

The discerning palate of our pal Bing is a thing of wonder, and to his extended family, such behaviour is just one of the reasons why we've become *'drawn in'* to what can only be termed...

'The World of Bing.'

Tim Harnden-Taylor

It's a Var, Var Better Place That I Go To...

Alison and I are back from our hols in the south of France and now we are back into our routine, which of course has the bonus of the Boy Bing once again managing to fit us into his busy week!

'So, guv, was it good in France?'

'Very nice, Bing, though I must admit I was rather lazy, and took things mighty easy.'

'Nothing new there then, guv.'

The Ruminations of Bing

'Oh, I say, that's a bit harsh.'

'Really, old poop? I mean, when I'm about 'Lyons', I get the impression life with you is hardly a blur.'

'Charming.'

'No offence, guv, but let's face it, the days of you dashin' and jumpin' about are but a distant memory...if, in fact, you ever did.'

There are times when the lad has a nasty way of reminding me that I'm not as fit as I once might have been. But time moves on, and for me, dashin' and jumpin' are somewhere back in the mists of time...now it's trundlin' and saunterin' and such like.

'Hello, his mind's wandering, which means I shall have to give him a *paff* to bring him back to earth.'

'Bingo, I am not deaf.'

'Hello, hello, he's back with us again. So, guv, give me a taste of what this France business is all about.'

'Well, Bing, when we are there, it is generally nice and warm. As we are not working, we tend to enjoy relaxing, and of course most of our day is spent outside, either out and about or lazing on the patio or by the pool.'

Tim Harnden-Taylor

'So why don't you do that here, guv?'

'Well, that's a good question, but I think it fair to say, we cannot always guarantee the weather in England, but down there, it's nearly always just right.'

'So where is it, guv?'

'It's in a region called The Var...in fact, you could say it's *Var from the madding crowd!* Ha-Ha!'

'I haven't a clue why you think that's funny, guv.'

'No? So why are you wagging your tail?'

'It seems to find you funny, guv, whereas up this end, I haven't a clue.'

'It's still wagging, Bing.'

'Okay, old poop, the truth is, when you make one of your funnies, you look so happy it makes me happy as well, even if I don't understand, and then of course my old wagger goes silly and then we both start laughing and neither of us knows why.'

'Fun, isn't it, Bing?'

'Yep...now, come on. Let's have a bit of squeaky ball chasing and perhaps a snack or four...'

'Three, Bing.'

'Well, it was worth a try, eh, guv?'

'Always worth a try, Bing...'

The Ruminations of Bing

Angela Lansbury Will Never Know...

The music for *Murder She Wrote* has caused my resting eyes to flicker open. They view the closing titles flying up the screen at such a rate, that I'll never know the name of the *'2nd Best Boy's Mate'!* I notice, too, my fellow snoozer lying at a most peculiar angle.

I'm never quite sure if the Boy Bing has been watching a programme, his shaggy eyebrows obscure his eyes at times.

'Well,' I venture. 'That episode will remain a mystery.'

'Very likely, guv, I'd imagine most of the programme before will have been lost to you as well.'

'No, no Bing, I know who the murderer was in...um...er... oh, dear.'

I receive a look, and yes, his eyes are in view!

Tim Harnden-Taylor

The day is one of steady rain. There hasn't been a drop of sunlight since early morning, and we are both extremely cheesed off. The grass needs cutting and a certain chap, no names, no pack drill, has been wondering why we haven't trundled up to the forest and enjoyed a really damp stroll!

The Boy Bing resettles on the settee and has another go at trying to tempt me out...

'Look, guv, it's starting to brighten up out there!'

'Bing, it's as dull and damp as it was an hour ago, in fact, it's even murkier than before.'

'I reckon your specs have misted up.'

My companion grumbles slightly as he rests his chin back down and wrinkles his nose at the 'box'.

'I suppose there's no sport on, guv?'

I flick to the various sports channels and the following comments are made:

'No, nope, cor, not that again, no, ski jumping without snow? Don't get me started about tennis without squeaky balls, seen it, nope...'

The Ruminations of Bing

His sudden dislike of all sport is based purely upon the need to get a certain old poop out of the house, and up into the forest. Even I'm not fooled for a moment.

Having carefully dismounted from the couch, he stretches, wanders to the garden window and looks disconsolately out at the stair-rods thundering down.

'Coo, I don't know, guv, a gentle 'scotch' mist, and you're not up for a trundle and such.'

I refuse to be drawn into the ruse and receive a scowl for my trouble.

A stroll to the kitchen finds my gloomy companion already sitting patiently next to the shelf whereon sits his snack tin. I receive a reminding cough as I pass.

'You fancy a snack, Bing?'

'Well, as I'm here and not out there, I s'pose I do.'

Tim Harnden-Taylor

A fresh cuppa is poured and the lad receives a snack or three. At least these are gracefully received.

Back to the lounge and as I sip my drink and settle down, I note the lad has assumed the upside-down position on the other couch...

'Best for viewing snooker, hey, Bing?'

I receive a low growl, followed by...

'Blooming weather.'

The Ruminations of Bing

Birds Of A Feather...

'Well, I never...and such.'

'Oi, guv, quick, quick, come and have a look!'

'What am I looking at, Bing?'

Tim Harnden-Taylor

'That lot up there! Put your specs on...'

'Bing, they're in the garden over the road too...'

'And ours!!!'

The Ruminations of Bing

'Duck down, guv, they're looking over here.'

'Oo'er, they're all on the lawn now...'

'Good heavens, old poop, they're having a blooming picnic!'

Tim Harnden-Taylor

'Well, if that doesn't take the biscuit!'

'Keep your voice down, guv, you're so noisy and blooming nosey!'

'I'll have you know, you called me, Bing!'

'M'mmm... what's that you said, guv?'

The Ruminations of Bing

From Green Baize To Greenwood...

'Well, I never.'

'Never what, guv?'

(Bing is watching snooker and hoping they will shortly, finally, introduce coloured balls that squeak!)

'M'mmm?'

'You're sounding puzzled, old poop.'

I've been scanning a local 'freebie' newspaper and wondering if anyone actually reads such things. Being sharp, I realise...in fact...*I* am*!*

'Sorry, Bing, I was wondering why yet another new restaurant is about to open in Lowtown. We seem to have an extraordinary number of eating establishments, betting offices and estate agents. Not to mention clothes, and phone shops. Oh, *and* Opticians!'

Tim Harnden-Taylor

...actually I fear this can be said for many a high street up and down our fair land. I then spend a few moments counting hairdressers, barbers, suntan and nail buffers etc. Oh, and slightly fewer banks and building societies than a few years back.

Naturally, to someone as level-headed as the Boy Bing, such establishments don't figure large in his world... although the *'pongs'* coming from local 'eateries' are, quite naturally, of interest.

A paw is rested on my knee, and I can see the lad's about to bring sense back to our day.

'Guv'ner, let it go. Just think, the day is bright, there's a lad before you in the mood to stroll. We *deserve* a trundle about the paths we love. Let's face it, apart from a few too many grey tails *(squirrels)*, the rest is nigh on perfect!'

'Well...'

The lad is off, out into the hall he trundles, and you and I know, by the time I catch up, he'll be sitting very neatly, next to the chair on which his lead rests.

Restaurants and so forth are very *'small beer'* when it comes to strolls with Bing. The path is dry, the hooter up front is working overtime, and here, being towed in his wake, comes an old poop with a silly smile on his face.

The Ruminations of Bing

We reach our little pond, look for ducks, who today are being particularly vociferous. Later, we trundle the banks of one of the *'meanders'* that trickle through this forest. Much later they will join the River Roding, which empties into the Thames and from there...our little world of Lowtown joins the world.

'Oi!'

I jump out of my reverie.

'Yes, Bing?'

'Still thinking of new shops?'

'No.'

'Hurrah!'

A pigeon clatters from forest floor to high beech branch.

'Crumbs, that's a real porker of a pigeon, Bing!'

'Um...I'd like to see you get up to a high branch from here, guv!'

'Charming!'

'Talking of snacks, guv...'

'Were we?'

Tim Harnden-Taylor

'Well, we are now, I would suggest.'

'M'mmmmm.'

'Anything you'd like to ask me, guv?'

'Snack, Bing?'

'Need you ask?'

A suitable stump is found, an old poop gets comfy, and...of course...

Snacks are served.

And through the trees, old Lowtown nestles.

Monks Have Habits... Bing Has Routines....And So Forth!

If ever there was a creature of habit, I think it would be fair, and pretty safe, to pop the Boy Bing at the summit of that particular term.

Routine is very much to his liking, and frankly any sudden changes in the daily round are to be frowned upon, particularly if the lad has decided the day should be just so and not thus...if you get my drift.

Recently, we have been enjoying extra time with Bing as there is a certain amount of building work going on at his residence! Most of the time, he is very happy with the change, as Tom and Angela and 'an Arthur' are here with us, and he has various areas that are regular snoozing spots within the confines of our house.

The problems seem to come when T and A have to pop out suddenly, and the lad is not part of the 'popping out' group.

Tim Harnden-Taylor

He stands, sits, and eventually lies by the front door, sniffing the air that passes under the bottom gap. Low growls have been heard, and on occasion an unearthly 'howl' will be generated, which receives an...

'Oh, Bing, they've only just popped out to pick up a few bits and pieces and so forth.'

'M'mmmm.'

'I realise you like to be involved with just about everything that goes on, but I'm pretty sure shopping is not high on your list of things to do.'

'M'mmmm.'

The hooter continues to sniff along the gap between mat and door.

'Well, I don't know about you, but I reckon I could do with a cuppa, and, just maybe, a snack.'

The word *cuppa* is ignored, but as the 'K' in *snack* is completed, his attention is on me.

'Snack, guv?'

'Certainly, Bing, certainly.'

I'm now wandering towards the kitchen and amazingly as I enter, the lad is already parked by the snack tin, in anticipation of the next few moments.

The kettle is turned on, and as it heats up, I prise open Bing's 'nosh' tin, and we go through the ritual of how the lad likes to have the snack delivered to him. I'm sure I've mentioned in the past that the lad has his own way with snacks and, unlike all the other dogs in the past, he is very, very deliberate in his eating methods.

Not for him the quick guzzling of any food proffered. The lad takes each offering and will often find a spot to 'park' it before receiving the next 'delight'. By the time I've made a coffee and settled at the table to sip it and maybe eat a slice

The Ruminations of Bing

of toast, Bing has (weather permitting) taken his goodies outside and quietly gone about the gentle *noshing of nosh!*

As I look out into the garden now, there he is, sitting very neatly and listening very, very carefully for the return of T and A and of course 'an Arthur'...the lad's ears pick up the shutting of car doors, and immediately he dashes back into the house and to the front door, head cocked to one side as he hears them arriving at the front door!

All is well once again, routine is back in rhythm with the lad.

The world of Bing can continue as he would wish it to be... well, until the next time!

Tim Harnden-Taylor

Sunday Morning Guests!

'And when I tell them...they never believe me...they never believe me!'

'Really, Bing, I'd just popped into the kitchen to get another coffee!'

'Hop on, guv, there's plenty of room for two!'

'I see that huge black bird is sitting on the gate post!'

The Ruminations of Bing

'Can you see him, guv?'

'Hello, he's up on the top of that roof now!'
'Bing!'
'Yes, guv?'

'I guess I could just about type with one finger...I can just about see the screen...'

Tim Harnden-Taylor

'Are you quite comfortable, Bing?'

'M'mmmmmm...?'

'I'll tell you what, let me move you and this chair over slightly and put another chair here...'

'Whatever, guv.'

'Some folk just don't believe me when I tell 'em about you, Bing...they think it's all part of my odd imagination...'

The Ruminations of Bing

Now Where Was I...?

It's hard to believe, I know, but my mind has, on occasion, been known to wander. I'm not sure whether this is an affliction or not. Certainly, from earliest years, I have had the capacity to disappear into another world, where I can find the most wandering thoughts extraordinarily interesting. I have, by necessity, accepted that this is part of 'my world' and therefore any attempt to keep its confines at arm's length is quite impossible.

For those that have bothered to glance at previous *Lines From My Forehead* and the exploits of a certain lad, none of this will come as any sort of surprise. The Boy Bing is a true phenomenon, who has graciously spent time with an aged codger, and attempted to engage the aforementioned wandering mind, and thus rescue the guv from procrastination!

The results, I fear, have been mixed. We cannot and certainly won't blame my canine companion. The task is, I fear, nigh on impossible but I'm terribly grateful for the efforts he continues to make.

I see, in his eyes, an eagerness that can never be dimmed. Affability is his watchword, and his enquiring mind has kept this old poop on his toes, more often than I care to mention.

Ah, there's the doorbell, which means the lad is about to start his day with me.

'Morning, Bing.'

'Wotcha, guv!'

My conversation with Tom is brief, as the lad trundles around the house, rather like an FBI agent checking security arrangements, prior to a Presidential visit! As we chat, the lad is now out in the back garden, sniffing out any recent activity.

Tim Harnden-Taylor

Tom calls out...

'Cheerio, Bing!'

This brings the lad back into the hall.

'See you later, Tom.'

The front door closes and for a few seconds, the lad remains seated, watching the silhouette depart, before dashing off to his day bed, where he awaits a couple of small Bonios from yours truly, prior to the start of the day's activities.

The Ruminations of Bing

'Well, Bing, did you have a good night's kip?'

'Not bad, guv, An Arthur was active a couple of times in the night, but fortunately he settled eventually, I think, but I'd already nodded off again.'

'You'll be glad to know, Bing, that there's snooker on the box today.'

'Lovely, lovely...any ski jumping?'

'Nope. The season has come to an end.'

'Crumbs, no snow, eh?'

'Something like that.'

So folks, the day has started, and who knows where we will end up!

Now really...where was I?

Tim Harnden-Taylor

My Particular 'Woad' To Recovery!

'Come on, keep up!'

I am out with my new personal trainer.

I have, I believe, mentioned, at least once before, that I'm a fair weather trundler. Whereas, dear reader, I'm happy to profess it might possibly have been one of my ancestors, who was happy to stand naked and painted blue, on the white cliffs of Dover, shaking a fist and hurling insults at Roman legions and their ships. This particular member of that ancient line would, I fear, now, not be up for that task!

No, as age starts to rest upon this old poop's brow, I'm more than happy to take a back seat when it comes to such histrionic outbursts. However, my personal trainer will brook no such protestations, and expects his new charge to at least make some sort of effort, given the necessity to rearrange and reduce my body mass index and...so forth, and...yes...suchlike!

By now, I'm sure you'll have realised, the Boy Bing has taken on this onerous task and at this moment is towing a panting idiot about the ancient confines of Lowtown's forest.

The Ruminations of Bing

'Let's face it, guv, there's no gain without pain.'

I mutter something. This, fortunately, is drowned by the clatter of a helicopter flying back to its base, close by The Owl – one of our ancient forest's delightful hostelries. I smack my lips at the thought of a foaming pint and receive a look of reproach from my coach!

'Stone me, Bing, I can't keep this pace up!'

Not for the first time this morning, I receive a glance, so laced with incredulity, that I'm forced to smile back lamely and toddle along with the appearance of 'joy'.

'Frankly, old poop, you have let yourself go. I've heard you tell of days, long past, when you were as packed full of energy as a young whippet!'

'Ah, yes, well...'

'Aged guv, I find it very hard to believe.'

'No, well...um, I do assure you that I was pretty fit once upon a time.'

'Once upon a time...sounds like the start of a fairy story.'

'M'mmm. Well, nevertheless in my defence, I can produce photographic evidence, clearly showing a lithe young Tim.'

We are taking a breather, and my PT is seated before me. Slowly, my breathing is returning to a fairly normal state.

I'm thinking it's payback time. After all, an aged poop has to make sure he remains 'top dog'!

'Now, Bing, as you know, it's now up to you to set an example, when it comes to dietary matters, and so I'm assuming you won't be requiring a snack or three at this juncture?'

'Think what you like, guv, but if you don't hand over the goodies, I'll bounce you!'

'Crumbs...'

'That's what I'm gonna make of my snacks!'

I am, I like to think, a fair minded sort of cove - and decide I have made my point...

...and meekly hand the goods over, receive a 'wink' as payment and prepare to 'lumber' on!

The Ruminations of Bing

It's All About Whether The Weather Is... Whatever!

I think it fair to say that the Boy Bing is of a very bright disposition, and rarely have I seen him grumpy. In short, if on the odd occasion he has appeared a tad grumpy, within seconds it is possible to lift his spirits and he's ready for anything.

I mention this because recently I strolled into the kitchen to refresh my coffee mug, to find the lad by the back door, peering out at the stormy day beyond.

'Fancy a snack, Bing?'

I received a sigh and my pal for the day continued his vigil by wrinkling his hooter of renown and sighing.

'Oh, Bing, we can't have this. I realise it's raining heavily, but I'm sure there must be something you would like to do?'

The lad 'huffed' a bit, and 'tupped' somewhat, and finally strolled over to me and gently received the proffered snack. This he carried to his daybed and placed it neatly before him.

Tim Harnden-Taylor

Ah, I thought, he's in one of those moods when he carefully collects his treats and neatly lines 'em up, until such time as he decides to 'nosh'!

'Will it ever stop raining, guv?'

'Good question, Bing. I'm afraid it looks as if this weather is certainly set in for the day.'

'Really, guv?'

'Well, I've lived in Lowtown for many years now and I do believe I can be relied on to give a pretty accurate state of the local weather, and I have to report that today is quite definitely a wet'un!'

The lad's head hung lower than before.

At this precise moment, as if to make me look a complete poop, the sun chose to pop its hat on and slide defiantly out from behind a very dark cloud! A rainbow gracefully arched the sky.

'Well, I'll be...'

'Blimey, guv, you're about as accurate as those folk on the box!'

'Weather forecasters?'

'Probabubbly.'

The Ruminations of Bing

'I don't, of course, have expensive computer programs to aid my forecasts, Bing.'

'M'mmm.'

By this point, the sun was positively beaming like a good'un, and my companion was pressing his hooter on a window pane, attempting to sniff the scene beyond.

I opened the back door and out he shot, trundling around the confines of the back garden, positively beaming at everything in sight.

Even the old poop was tempted out, and shortly after, was pulling up some of last year's dead plants, which should have been dealt with months ago...actually, now they were much easier to pull up and pop into the weed bag.

'Thank you, Bing, I think they are quite safe in there.'

The lad does like to inspect anything placed in the bag for disposal.

'Can't help it, guv, I just have to give 'em a good *hootering* before you pop them back!'

Gardening with Bing is like most other events with him, decidedly different.

Tim Harnden-Taylor

The day cheered up.

It was as if Bing could never be gloomy...

Snacks were consumed...

Which, as I'm sure you will agree - is as it should be!

The Ruminations of Bing

Not Quite An O'Henry Tale...

We have, in the past, touched on the uneasy truce between a hoover called Henry and a chap called Bing.

I've been trundling around the hall and front rooms with the former, whilst the latter has strategically withdrawn upstairs, to check on who's wandering up and down the street. (I say this, but am aware that, from time to time, a certain head peeps from the return landing, *'tut-tuts'* and returns to his advanced scouting position.)

Hoovering is a job that has to be done, and even the Boy Bing is quite happy to stretch luxuriantly upon a freshly vacuumed rug!

Time passes and finally the 'roar' from Henry subsides and peace return to 'Lyons'.

Tim Harnden-Taylor

'Thank goodness for that, guv!'

I have completed my task and Henry is now occupying his *parc fermé* slot, and Bing is giving him a suspicious sniff.

'Cor, he's a noisy type and such.'

'Well, Bing, he has a job to do, and quite frankly, sucking up dust, fluff and so forth is a task best left to those who thrive on such deeds.'

Bing thrusts a wrinkled noise in the direction of his protagonist and wanders away with a nonchalant air, and at long last, I can enjoy a mug of coffee and...

'Ah-hum.'

A throat is cleared.

'Ah, Bing, can I help you?'

'As it happens, old poop, indeed you can.'

'I see.'

'Do you, guv? I have to say I'm surprised.'

'Really?'

'Well, I can see the tin, old fruit, but the contents are still within it, and not within me!'

The Ruminations of Bing

'I take it you'll be thinking of a snack?'

'Or three, guv, or three.'

I have long been wondering just when a snack or two became three, but dare not speak of such matters to you know who, as the three could easily become four!

I have been told on more than one occasion, that, to put it bluntly, I'm an easy touch which I find quite hurtful, as I can be quite...um...er...determined...I feel sure.

'Oi!'

'What?'

'I said *Oi*!'

'Do you know, Bing, I'm sure it's not the done thing to *Oi!* a chap who is in the process of getting 'nosh' for the other chap?'

'Guv, I was merely trying to tug you back into the present as you had one of those looks on your face, that means you've gone *missing*.'

'Oh, I say.'

'No, guv, I say, and you do...get it?'

Somewhere, I'm sure I've read, it is vital that, in our relationships with others, we should, when required, remind other parties just who is top dog! I'm thinking this is indeed such an occasion and that now is the time to...

'Oi!'

'Oh sorry, Bing, what was I doing...'

'N-O-S-H!'

Nosh is handed over and coffee drunk.

Tim Harnden-Taylor

Food For Thought....And So Forth and Such Like

It is a blustery day. Out in the garden, the hairs on the Boy Bing's back are blowing like small feathers, and the '*hooter*' of renown is vertical and sniffing like a good'un. Naturally, it's a day that hounds find particularly invigorating, as sounds and scents arrive up the mighty snozzle from here, there and just about everywhere. This means the lad's brain is working overtime, noting each smell and cataloguing what each one is.

At such a time, I find it useful to let the boy enjoy this 'joy', for frankly no sensible conversation can be had whilst the '*hooter*' is thus occupied!

The whole operation is quite interesting to watch, for the keen observer will note that quite often the tip of the lad's tongue is poked out, as if the need to 'taste' the scent is also required.

The Ruminations of Bing

Occasionally, this performance is halted, when the lad spots a nosy squirrel observing him, or pigeon, or a largish bird wanders across the lawn behaving as if the grass is their property. The birds receive a deep 'woof' and a trundle in their general direction if the 'woof' is unheeded. Squirrels, of course, just carry on twitching their noses and flicking their tails. At this point, Bing will choose to ignore them by turning his back and continuing with his sniffing, or as he is wont to call it, 'hootering the environs!'

In the kitchen, I'm putting together a spot of lunch. Each opening of the fridge door or cupboard is picked up by the lad's 'earflaps' and my progress duly noted. The scrape of a chair leg will alert Bing that it is time to investigate the fare on the table.

This is usually done by casually sauntering in and looking mildly surprised that it is lunchtime already. Of course, if the smells received are those of strong cheeses or, let us say, ham, then his ability to look nonchalant is severely tested. For the lad, the King of cheeses is a honking piece of Roquefort or ripe Brie, and dare one admit, for such a 'bon vivre', the delicate flavour of a Dairylea triangle. This latter delight is used for disguising any pills the lad has been prescribed. (Just between you and me, the Boy Bing is ignorant of such matters, and shall remain so. The prospect of making him 'take his medicine' is impossible to comprehend but for Mr Kraft's delightful invention!)

'Ah, is it lunchtime already, guv?'

'Yup.'

The eyes and hooter are observing me from the other side of the table. Ears are pricked and head leans first one way and then the other, as a cracker loaded with cheese makes its way to my mouth.

'Um...any chance of a spot of lunch for a certain chap that is waiting *ever so* patiently over here?'

I start loading up another bit of cracker, whilst appearing to be interested in a magazine next to me.

'It's quite extraordinary, guv, did you know that long, long ago...'

I continue to look interested in an article about the correct way to make one's eyes up!

'Yes, long, long ago...so long ago that you were but a lad...'

I am not going to be lured into conversation with Bing. I know, somehow, he will con me into parting with nosh.

'Certain Kings, Emperors and many a Po...po...pote...'

'Potentate?'

'That's the geezer, guv, lived in the fear of being poisoned by their beloved subjects.'

'M'mmm.'

I try to look interested in an advert for improving my skin and lifting any bags that may have formed under my eyes.

'So, guv...'

(You have to admire the lad's perseverance.)

'They employed folk who'd have a taster of their guv's

The Ruminations of Bing

nosh, risking life and limb, thus ensuring the fare wasn't poisoned and the long life of said noble gaffer!'

It's no good. The lad has got my attention, but I resolve to remain strong.

'So, Bing, just how did you acquire this extraordinary info?'

'Well, old poop, we don't all watch sport, comedy and endless repeats of *Midsomer Murders*.'

'Oh, I say, that's not fair.'

'Well, I only speak as I find, guv.'

'All this still doesn't answer the question, Bing.'

'Oh, it was on one of the History type channels, I find 'em mighty interesting.'

'Really?'

'Very, very...um, very inter...should I not just have a taster of that latest succulent morsel, guv, just in case?'

My eyes narrow, for once I have the higher moral ground.

'And who would it be, Bingo, that would be attempting to poison this particularly minor potentate?'

'Ah, there you have me, guv. I am but a humble food taster-in-waiting, and not privy to such matters. Not for me the corridors of power, not for me the machinations of would-be power seekers or pretenders to the throne...no, not for this lad the glory that was Rome etc, etc.'

'I see.'

'No, I'm merely available to risk life and limb so that certain old puffers can nosh safely.'

'Well...?'

The lad suddenly appears at my side of the table and gives me a most winsome look.

'What about a snack or...'

Tim Harnden-Taylor

'Three, guv?'

'Well...?'

'You know it makes sense. Besides, all this chat has left me a tad peckish!'

The snacks are unloaded from their tin...and then it occurs to me.

'Perhaps, Bing, it would be apposite that I should test 'em, for it would not do for me to be the chap that ended the career of one such as you?'

'Cor, you don't half talk a load of twaddle, guv. Now, hand 'em over or I shall be forced to bounce you!'

'Oh, I say...'

Call me slow, and doubtless you will, but it was a full ten minutes before I remembered it was Bing who had bought up the whole subject of food testing! By then, it was too late, he not only had had the better of me (once again) but was now busy rolling in a sun-filled spot, prior to a quick 'forty wags'!

The Ruminations of Bing

Blow, Blow, Thou Winter Wind, Thou Art Not So Unkind...

'Cor, it's a bit draughty, Bing!'

'Is it?'

The lad is standing in front of me, with fur being whistled by an extremely windy day.

For reasons known only to those that know, Bing has managed to tempt me away from the warm confines of 'Lyons' to our present location – a track within our local forest.

'Frankly, Bing, I do believe Shackleton and his fellow polar explorers could have used such a day as this, to acclimatise to the rigours of the South Pole!!'

'Blimey, guv, it's little more than a gentle puff of a breeze!'

'Puff of a breeze? Puff of a breeze??'

'Certainly, old poop, certainly.'

'I'm sorry, but if this is your idea of a puff of breeze, I should hate to attempt to survive what you would call a stiff-ish zephyr!'

The boy is not listening, he's far too busy examining a rotting tree trunk and its surrounds.

'I think it might be a good idea if we trundle down to the pond and get out of this gale!!!'

This suggestion appeals to the lad, and off we set, weaving our way between beech trees and holly bushes. Fortunately, as we descend, the wind seems to lessen, and speaking as an old poop, I'm a lot happier.

This does not last.

Across a little bridge and around the last twist of the path and...there is the blooming wind again!

The Ruminations of Bing

'Stone the crows, Bing, this is ridiculous!'

'M'mmm?'

'Oh, please do not *M'mmm* me, this really is the end!'

'End of what, guv?'

Teeth chattering and nose running, I rummage through my pockets and finally manage to blow my nose!

'Steady, guv, you'll frighten the ducks!'

'Ducks?'

'Certainly, guv, certainly.'

'Bing, they seem to be being blown over the water, those that are silly enough to expose themselves to the elements.'

'It's the ducks playing America's Cup, guv!'

There are times when I realise the *World of Bing* is either to be embraced or ignored.

Folks, one look from the lad's eager eyes and wagging tail pops me straight into his *world*, and as we start the stroll home, the wind fairly whistles around us, as if it's in full agreement!

Tim Harnden-Taylor

Letting Sleeping Dogs...?

I like to think I'm the sort of chap who isn't a creature of habit. Sadly, as the years pass, I'm coming to realise the opposite is nearer the truth. This is not to say I can't be cajoled into a sudden change of plans, but generally the weekly routine is not too bad.

As a 'for instance', I was sitting at the kitchen table, sipping coffee, when it suddenly occurred to me that something was missing. I went through the time-honoured routine of patting my shirt pocket, and then my head - usually a good way of locating glasses - and having reassured myself that they were to hand, should the need arise, I was still aware that something was most definitely missing.

The sharper amongst you will have already guessed there was no Bing about!

Meanwhile I, and any of you still as slow as me, continued to scratch my head and mutter 'ummm?'

I wandered into the study and half-heartedly began wading through another pile of circulars, bills and statements, hoping something more interesting would turn up.

Some hopes!

Further down another pile, I discovered a CD that had somehow wandered into the bills. As our musical tastes might not concur, I shan't waste your time with a description of this particular work, suffice to say I was shortly after, listening to the wonderful opening bars of Bruckner's *4th Symphony*.

(Sorry for wasting your time!)

My comfort zone just about survived the 1st movement, but as it was coming to a close, the feeling of something missing wandered back into the cavern, which, for the sake of decency, I shall call my brain.

The Ruminations of Bing

It was no good, I was definitely not at ease and decided a few minutes trundling a tune or two out of the piano might do the trick.

It was sometime later, whilst pouring a cup of coffee, that I caught up with the rest of you, and remembered that the lad was missing!

As yet, I haven't quite entered the realm of complete forgetfulness. The lad had arrived earlier and had taken himself off into the garden to do a 'patrol' of the bounds, and I had wandered off to...um...well, do whatever it was I had in mind to do.

Bing is very much a lad of habit, and usually by now, he would've wandered in and pointedly made a remark about the passage of time and so forth, and shouldn't the old poop be thinking about mid-morning snacks...and such?

A quick stroll around the garden showed no sign of the lad, and so I wandered upstairs, assuming that I would find him standing on a chest and looking out of a bedroom window.

Not there.

I was beginning to wonder if he had taken up one of his napping stations under the piano, when I heard a sound coming from another bedroom. There the lad was discovered, out like a light, and as snug as a bug in the proverbial rug!

'Bing!'

Tim Harnden-Taylor

'M'mmmmwassat?'

'Bing, you'll get us both shot!'

'It's luverly, guv, I'm surprised you don't spend longer snoozing here.'

This was not the time to harp on about my poor sleeping habits. The lad is well known for leading me away from the topics in hand by engaging me in explanations that gently lead me away from...whatever it was I was about to speak about.

'Bing?'

'Yes, old poop?'

'I think you and I should be downstairs and...'

'Snacking, guv?'

'Well...'

'I don't mind if I do, guv, I don't mind if I do!'

Like a blur, he descended the stairs...I closed the bedroom door and, I think wisely, decided to draw a veil over this episode.

'C'mon, guv, I'm starving!'

The Ruminations of Bing

Dairylea & Pineapple Poll

We have not been well.

This is not the royal 'we' but reference to the lad and the old poop.

Naturally, at this time of year, it can't be surprising for the old huff-and-puffer, but the young chap, whose days are spent making the most of each moment, has also been under the weather.

The Vet has been consulted, and a course of antibiotics should do the trick.

(I'm convinced that a surfeit of snow could be a possible cause!)

I arrived home yesterday to find Bing slightly unsure of a guest who's staying with us for a few days. Normally, the lad is a mighty fine greeter of visitors, but now and then, the 'guest' has something about them that the lad finds odd, and therefore he is on his guard.

'Hello, guv, how yer going?'

'I'm going pretty well, considering everything and such. How are you, old fruit?'

'I'm finding the Dairylea diet is taking effect, and I'm pretty chipper, old poop.'

Tim Harnden-Taylor

Dairylea is the 'magic lozenge' that a certain young fellow believes to be the panacea and none of his pals is going to mention the added contents held within!

'I see old JR has arrived.'

'M'mm...crumbs, guv, I thought you were a tad *upsy-daisy-and-such* but frankly, this here geezer is mighty odd.'

'Really, Bingo, he is rather nice and I hear he has been supplied with digestive biscu...'

My sentence trailed away, as the lad popped off to check JR out! On arrival in the lounge, I find JR and the lad the best of pals.

'Careful, chaps, you'll have Alison after you if she finds a certain chap is being given unscheduled treats.'

'Honest, guv, they're mere noggins, nothing over the top.'

JR and I shake hands and Bing pops out to the kitchen to see if a new cuppa is on the way for his new pal – oh, and a further supply of a digestive or three!

And...he is back with a 'gift' for the new guest (on this occasion a 'squeaky' bone). JR looks totally mystified (he's a cat man) and the lad wanders off, happily unaware of the surprised expression on our guest's face.

JR is Alison's old *pas de deux* teacher, and those who know him are used to his rather eccentric manner. Originally an Ipswich lad, he was Russian-ballet trained, and thus over the decades has developed his own vocabulary, which takes a while to tune into!

Bing has decided that he is 'fine' and therefore the next few days should be fun, if at times confusing.

Our DVD player will be running overtime, as John has come armed with various rare ballet clips, on several disks. I've recently purchased copies of *La Fille Mal Gardée* with Nadia Nerina, David Blair and Stanley Holden! (Not forgetting Alexander Grant) Another DVD has *The Lady*

The Ruminations of Bing

and the Fool and Pineapple Poll (the latter with David Blair and Stanley Holden)...I last saw these when I was just a lad...so you can guess how ancient they are!

And the Boy Bing?

I fear he will not be too impressed...he will slumber through them all...and his dreams will be full of warmer days and the possibility of dragging the aged chump through the forest!

Roll on Spring, please!

Tim Harnden-Taylor

To Sleep, Perchance To Dream...

There are times, it has to be said, when a certain young lad requires correction!

It also has been said, and it is very likely true, that I'm a *'soft touch'* when it comes to being charmed into acquiescing to Bingo's behaviour.

Call it fanciful, but from time to time, he can take on the air of a defence council, pleading a good cause (generally his own!). Well, let's face it, his long ears can appear quite 'Crown Court' like, and his confident air and little nods and winks can really charm the easily led. (Me.)

I understand it has been suggested (by some) that many of the photos published of the lad himself, have been *'set up'* and, charming as some of them are, they appear to be *'posed'!*

The Ruminations of Bing

Untrue!

What you see is what you get. The Boy Bing trundles through his day in his own inimitable fashion, quite oblivious of being *'different'*.

This preamble, folks, is by way of an advance warning to what follows.

Not content with our couch and its regular appearance and state, the lad, with great effort, managed to alter the design and find perfection...

...that was, until Alison discovered him, and decided enough was quite enough!

(Didn't stop her from taking a snap first!!)

As Bing would no doubt say... *'I rest m'case, me Lud!'*

Tim Harnden-Taylor

When It's Raining, It Must Be...GAMES DAY!!

There was heavy rain outside, and the old poop was not for venturing out! Like many a youngster, Bing was bored! I therefore attempted to teach the lad some new games. It must be said he's a quick learner, and what he sometimes lacks in skill, he more than makes up for with enthusiasm!

We have a large box in which we keep various items of interest to visiting grandchildren, etc. Bing decided it might be an idea to unpack some of these items to see what they were all about 'and so forth and such like, guv'.

The extra-large Lego bricks were of interest, and he waited most patiently while I built a large tower. On completion, he sauntered over and prodded it with his hooter. As it tumbled, he shot off and sat at a distance looking entirely innocent. (7/10)

Next, various musical toys were discovered, and set in motion.

'M'mmm, they're mighty noisy, ain't they, guv?'

'Glad you agree, old chap. I must admit, after a few minutes, I can easily tire of their chirpy chiming!' (3/10)

He was mystified by the slinky spring that trickled down the staircase but could not go back by itself.

'Ah, that's gravity, Bingo.'

'Well, you can tell Gravity that I'll be even more impressed when he can trundle up the stairs as well!'

'M'mmm...' (5/10)

The lad was quite disconcerted with 'the racer' - this would pick up speed across the room but appeared quite unable to dodge anything in its path. Various spectacular crashes

The Ruminations of Bing

ensued, causing the lad much concern and mystification at its inability to steer and alter direction. (4/10)

Fuzzy Felt did not appeal.

The card game Snap degenerated into a hopeless scrummage as the lad called 'Snap!' every time a new card was turned!

Even *more* degeneration occurred as I attempted to explain the niceties of Twister which rapidly descended in to 'duff the old poop up!' (8/10)

(Refreshments were had.)

Rummaging in the box continued.

Posting letters into a letterbox and pushing various shapes into another box held no interest, whilst my attempt to play a small xylophone was greeted with…

'Stick to the piano, guv.' (2-3/10)

Man of course, has invented various toys and games to keep the young entertained, and yet how often do we say, '*I think they had more fun with the large box it came in*'?

As for the Boy Bing, large boxes are 'great, guv!'…although they might get a bit of a chewing.

Finally, during a pause the lad said, 'So, aged bloater, how about I Spy?'

It was time, I thought, for another cuppa and possibly a Bonio for the lad.

'**SNAP!** guv.'

Tim Harnden-Taylor

One Hundred Not Out!

The closing credit music for *New Tricks* was fading when a certain chap deposited himself off a settee, stretched and gave me a puzzled look.

'Well, that was all a bit mystifying.'

'Really, Bing?'

'Certainly, guv, certainly.'

A yawn follows and then another stretch. I wait for the next sentence with bated breath.

Nothing.

Dare I ask the lad what was so mystifying? Might whatever follows be as incomprehensible as the mystification?

Silence.

It's no good, the lad has appealed to my inquisitive nature.

'What was so mystifying, Bing?'

'Oh, well, I suppose it was nothing, really.'

'Really?'

The Ruminations of Bing

'It's just that...'

The lad's voice trailed away and a wistful expression reposed upon the noble brow.

Silence.

'Bing!'

'M'mmm?'

'Stone me, what was it that was so mystifying?'

'Ah, well, it was nothing, really.'

I know I'm not a particularly patient man. However, I try to make a special point of adopting the demeanour of a kindly uncle when with the lad...but there are times...

'You see, guv, I was merely wondering when that chap from *Minder* joined the police force?'

'So, you followed the plot quite easily?'

'Well, it wasn't really that twisty, was it? Not as tricky as one of Inspector Thingummy's.'

'Morse?'

'That's the fellow.'

'I see.'

'Jolly good.'

Actually, I didn't really, but let's face it, I really didn't want the lad to get too obsessed with why George Cole's minder is now a policeman!

I'm sorry but the world of Bing is quite complicated enough, thank you very much!!

Tim Harnden-Taylor

Pep Talks...And Their Worth

'The thing is, Bing...'

'Yes, guv?'

'I'm not absolutely sure of the numbers, but I would certainly think they run into scores of times.'

'Really, aged sage?'

'Oh, yes, definitely, up in the hundreds, I would say.'

'Good heavens, that sounds quite a lot, even to a chap of my elk.'

'Ilk, I think you mean, Bing.'

'If you say so, guv, you're the araldite one.'

'Araldite?...oh, you mean *erudite*?'

'If it means learned? Then you're the shop for it.'

'Well...I'm not sure about that, however...um...er...'

'You were saying "the thing is", I believe, ol' poop.'

'Was I?'

The Ruminations of Bing

'Indubitabubbly.'

Was I? Was I indeed...m'mmm? (I stare into space...a particular trait of mine, observed by more than one teacher long ago.)

'Oh, yes, that's it. As I was saying, young fellow, I can't tell you how many times I've told you not to clamber over the furniture. It's surely sufficient that you're able to snooze on either one of two couches, but making a conversion job as you do, from time to time, is frowned upon.'

'I see.'

'But do you? Let's face it, I am not the only person to have admonished you.'

'Well, that's certainly very true, ol' Mr Grumpy.'

'Why are you unable to observe this fairly minor rule?'

I receive a stare from the lad, not dissimilar to the ones observed by my teachers long ago.

'Well, Bing?'

(I'm now starting to sound like my teachers of long ago.)

'Well, oh, mighty geezer and controller of the snack tin, it's like this. When a chap like me suddenly feels in need of a 'lights out' moment or three, he naturally gravitates to known surfaces affording the most delightful prospect of a quick Z'zzz.'

'And?'

'As you know, guv, it can't be denied that, when it comes to comfy-ville, this lad before you is inclined to seek perfection.'

'Don't I know it!'

'Therefore, at such moments, all other considerations cease to be…considered.'

'Well?'

'That's just it, oh seeker of justice and truth, a hound's well-being kicks in, so to speak, and you discover me in this current predicament.'

'As usual, Bing, your reasoning is interesting, but fails to take into consideration the need to observe some hard and fast rules.'

'I see. Although I feel I ought to point out one particularly salient point.' (Where he gets such words from is a total mystery.)

'That being, Bing?'

'I am a hound, guv.'

'I see.'

'Do you, oh, aged poop?'

'Well, of course…however…'

'Good heavens, is that the time?'

'Time, time?'

'Certainly, guv, certainly.'

'It's 11 o'clock Bing.'

'Stone me and so forth…have you not popped the kettle on and such?'

The Ruminations of Bing

'Um...well...er...not yet.'

'That is very unlike you, I have to say. I mean to say, an aged poop might be able to behave like a camel, but chaps like me need their mid-morning snack.'

'Ah.'

'How's your memory for snack tin finding?'

'I'm not entirely decrepit, Bing.'

But I'm talking to a wagging tail disappearing in the direction of the kitchen.

I remake the couch and wander to where the snack tin and waiting hound wait. Naturally, any hope of my little pep talk having made any sort of lasting impression on the lad was...and why am I surprised by this? A complete waste of ...

...time and suchlike.

Tim Harnden-Taylor

The Missing Link....And Other Items!

For those of you who've wandered these pages, strolls...

'And so forth, guv?'

'Quite, Bing.'

'And such like?'

'Yes...now, where was I?'

The lad has already wandered off to enquire within and without...

For those of you who've wandered these pages, strolls and 'moments' over the last few years, I'm sure by now you may have decided that the Boy Bing is the catalyst by which our time together has served to re-sharpen this particular old noodle's ability to 'keep up!'

On the whole, taken by and large and up and down and all other directions...

'You still tripe-writing, guv?'

'Um...well, actually, as it happens...'

'May I ask if you're the geezer that has whipped me new squeaky ball?'

The Ruminations of Bing

'Bing!'

'Look, old wheezy-bonce, you're just the sort of vague trundling old poop, who forgets where he was when he last had a chap's flavourite Squeaker!'

'Bing, I am not forgetful!'

'Found your other glasses, yet?'

'Which ones?'

'Ah, so there's more than one pair missing, eh?'

'No, not really...just...momentarily...out of position.'

'And yer mobile, Kindle, mug of coffee going cold somewhere...need I go on?'

'Well, I...I...'

But he is gone. New scents have been received by the wondrous hooter, and their call leads him away.

As I was saying, our relationship could appear a tad odd to some. (I'm sure not you.) I like to think that I've generally managed the partial education of Bing quite well, given that as a hound, he has a slightly different view of things...

'You'll be pleased to hear, old bloater, that I've relocated the whereabouts of me yellow orb, and have discovered you left it in the raised flowerbed.'

'Me?'

'Yep-p-p-p-p!'

'I left it in the raised flowerbed?'

'He's quick, you know.'

'Why would I do that, Bing?'

'Mine is not to reason why, old wrinkle chin, mine is but to dig and dive.'

'Bing, I find it hard to believe I would take your pill outside and pop it in the raised flowerbed?'

'I know, it's odd, isn't it, guv? You really do some rummy things.'

'But, but, but...'

But he's gone again, padding off down the hall with his 'pal'.

Despite these moments, we rub along mighty well, although I believe I really must take him in hand and try and introduce a modicum of responsibility into his day to day routine.

Where he gets this peculiar behaviour from, I have no idea ...

The Ruminations of Bing

Now He Is Four

It's someone's Birthday...but you would never guess who?

I've just been greeted by Bing!

The lad is positively fizzing with bonhomie. Little respect is shown to our settees as he leaps and bounces on them both, whilst lapping the lounge several times, before finally diving headlong on settee number one. This extraordinary performance is completed by burrowing his head under a cushion.

'And a good morning to you, Bing.'

His *'wagger'* is almost a blur, and up pops the slightly dishevelled head with beaming countenance.

'Wotcha, guv, you'll never guess...'

'That it's your Birthday?'

'Swipe me, how did you know?'

'Well, strangely enough, your name appears on our Birthday Calendar for this very day.'

'Well, as you would say, guv, slap my thigh and stack me vitals!'

Tim Harnden-Taylor

Note to self - I really must watch what I say before Bing. He is liable to blurt out just about anything to anyone.

'So, a Birthday is on the same day each year, oh, fount of all whatsits?'

'That's the idea, yes.'

'Next, I suppose you're going to tell me how old I am?'

'Well, you are four, Bing.'

'Oh, well, now you're just showing off, old poop.'

'Not really, Bing, you are four because four years ago today, you first appeared before an unsuspecting world.'

'So, if I'm four...?'

I'm dreading what comes next...

'You, old ancient puffer, must be hundreds and hundreds of years old. In fact, you're so old, you probably don't really know how old you are, eh?'

Four years of Bing and I've learnt when to give up.

'Probably, Bing.'

'Quite, quite, old wheezer.'

'My real problem is, Bing...'

'Yes, guv?'

'If I'm as old as, um, er, well, Methuselah, can I remember where any special Birthday snacks and treats might be?'

'Guv, I'm sure your thuselah, whatever that is, isn't so ancient that you'll have forgotten. I could of course apply my thuselah to the problem, assuming that it is a *hooter*-based chappie.'

Another note to self – don't complicate matters with words like Methuselah. Goodness knows who Bing will insult, by dropping such an ancient into his conversation.

I receive a nudge just below the knee.

The Ruminations of Bing

'Ah, you're still with us, then?'

'For the moment, Bing.'

'Well, come on, old trundler, let's get cracking on finding the special treats for the lad, eh?'

'Certainly, Bing, certainly.'

'After all, it'd be nice to have before I'm five!'

I receive a wink and he trundles off into the study...the *'hooter of renown'*, of course...

...knew exactly where they would be all along.

Tim Harnden-Taylor

The Moving Pen Writes And, Having Writ, Moves…Um…On…And So Forth

'You're a funny old poop, guv.'

'And good morning to you, Bing.'

'Well, I mean to say, I make all this effort to come and visit, and by use of my winsome charm, tempt and distract you…and if all others fail…cajole, nay, inveigle you from your inertia, up and out into the awaiting day, and all you do is sit there scratching at that bit of paper!'

Not for the first time am I feeling that, although he insists my old Roget's Thesaurus is no more than a convenient step up onto the 'viewing chair', there's a lot more to it.

'As it happens, Bing, I was, um, er…'

'Shuffling paper, guv?'

'I was actually looking for a ruler, when I discovered this old Shaeffer pen, nestling amidst boxes of staples to staplers I no longer have (I think), treasury tags, reinforcement rings and assorted labels.'

'Blimey, guv, it's a blooming Aladdin's cave of stationery wotsits you have in them there drawers…and such.'

The Ruminations of Bing

'M'mmmm.'

'So, what's this shaver all about then?'

'Shaeffer? Ah, yes, well, back in the old days...'

'Don't tell me...when you were a boy?'

'Indeed, Bing, I once was a boy.'

'Well, I'm not one to quibble, but frankly, old poop, it's blooming hard to believe you were ever a boy...'

'Nevertheless, Bing, I was!'

'M'mmmm.'

'At school, having mastered the pencil, we moved on to the pen and ink. These were what we called dip-in pens with ink-wells.'

'Not quills?'

'NO! Bingo, I'm not that old!'

'Keep yer mop on, guv, if you say so.'

'I do, young Bing, I most definitely do. Now, where was I?'

'Dipping your pen in an ink thingy...'

'Well...'

'Whatever, guv.'

'Um...well, eventually, I graduated to a fountain pen, probably a Parker, or a Platignum.'

'You've lost me, guv, but carry on.'

'I don't think I ever had a Shaeffer, but this is mighty fine, so I'm just about to fill it full of ink and see if it still writes.'

'I see.'

'Ink...ink...I know I've got some somewhere. Ah, here we are, I've got Quinck Royal Blue, or Stephens'...Green.'

'Cor, green ink, guv, why have you got that?'

Tim Harnden-Taylor

'Do you know, I have no idea at all.'

'Now, there's a surprise.'

'Right, so I pull this little lever out and...yes, it's sucking ink up inside itself.'

'Fascinating, guv.'

Is there a hint of irony in the lad's voice?

'Now, let's see if it still writes...Oh, yes, look at that, it's as smooth as anything...'

> *Dear Bing, this is a note to you, showing the delights of using a quality pen. I think you can't fail to be impressed by its ability to glide effortlessly across...*

'Oh, blast, it's poured ink all over the page...'

'Blimey, guv, your fingers are covered in ink-well, and such.'

'Must be a cross-nib.'

'It probably is angry, guv, you haven't used it in years!'

I debate whether to explain further, but frankly soap and water seem more important just now.

'So that's why it's called a fountain pen, old poop?'

'M'mmm?'

'Well, it cascaded over that page like a good'un.'

'U'mmm...'

'I guess it's back to the pencil for you, guv?'

I receive a wink, and the lad receives a snack or two!

The pen returns to its former position, nestling amidst...

The Ruminations of Bing

Scents and Insensibility!

When it comes to 'hooters', the one that completes the snout of the Boy Bing can be described as a sensitive piece of apparatus, beautifully tuned to all the possible scents that are missed by us mere mortals!

This day, we have been making particularly slow progress along the pavement leading to the forest, where, history states, Elizabeth I hunted. To corroborate this, her hunting lodge resides across the trees towards North Chingford.

We definitely won't be travelling that far today!

This morning, for once, the lad is being unexpectedly slow in his progress, and I'm enjoying the stately pace we're making. The 'hooter' of renown is being extraordinarily thorough in its research. Various types of grasses and suchlike are obviously affording delightful odours to the receiving 'conk'!

Finally, we have reached the slope that'll gain us access to our usual entry point into the forest of Epping. I'm relieved that again, we are taking this at a gentle stroll, the 'nose' in front taking as much care as a minesweeper!

'So, Bing, what is it that you're finding so invigorating this merry morn?'

I receive a nod of recognition but no words.

'Is it the flowers, the grasses or that newly mown lawn, perchance? Could it possibly be, young lad, the breeze wafting delicate odours from trees and shrubs?'

Tim Harnden-Taylor

I'm starting to feel quite Keats or Tennyson like, as I search for more piquant phrases to capture the joy of this scene. Suddenly the 'snozzle' is thrust into the lower realms of the privet hedge on one side of the path.

Muffled comments such as 'Ah, yes, this is it' and 'I can't quite get at it' waft up from the two thirds of hound I can see.

'Bing, are you all right?' Slowly, dare I say reluctantly, the lad reverses out and sits, 'hooter' wrinkling in my direction.

'Guv, it's an absolute corker of a pong!'

'Pong, Bing? Surely pong is really not the most suitable epithet for the delights afforded us this bright October day?'

'Well, old poop, flowers and grass are one thing, but the scents coming off that barbecue through there are a delightful combination of charcoal, delicately merged with bangers, burgers and suchlike!'

Disappointment was clearly etched upon my visage. I felt rather like a balletomane who, having sat waiting with great expectation, is suddenly served up with a large navvy clumping his way through a grotesque account of the *Dance of the Sugar Plum Fairy*.

The Ruminations of Bing

My disappointment was observed by the lad, who gave me a wink and said, 'Guv, I am, after all, a hound, and there are certain matters I'm afraid an old poop like you will never understand.'

'Oh?'

'Yes, it's true, old huff and puff. You, as soon as a touch of warmth is felt in the air, will wax lyrical about the joys of any season.'

'Yes?'

'Certainly, guv, certainly. Whereas chaps like me have centuries of specialist breeding, meaning our hooters are our livelihood.'

'Livelihood?' (I was losing the thread here.)

'Yes.'

My imbecilic gaze was duly noted, and the lad pressed on.

'Let us say, for the sake of argument, that Good Queen Bess was clattering around here, sitting side-saddle upon her trusty steed. Now, during the chase, various game birds and such have been felled with hawks and arrows and such, and we hounds are sent out to bring 'em in.'

'M'mmm.'

Tim Harnden-Taylor

'Now picture the scene, guv...let me, as the bard would say, *on your imaginary forces work*. What would Her Majesty's reaction be if a chap like me came trundling back with a mouthful of buttercups or cow parsley and said... "*Oh, Queeny, ain't these sweet smelling nosegays a delight?*"'

'Ah.'

'Ah, indeed, guv! Cor she'd say, "It's straight to the Tower for you, me lad!"'

'I see.'

'Replace the game birds with the scent from a barbecue or old takeaway and there you have it!'

'I see.'

'Do you, guv?'

'I do, Bing.'

'Don't be disappointed, old poop, remember I too like smelling flowers and so forth, but...'

His words faded away for we had entered the ancient forest. Here we started our gentle promenade, birds twittering as we strolled between the trees, whose earlier relatives, long, long ago...had looked upon a Sovereign's progress.

ABOUT THE AUTHOR

Born in London NW8 and now living towards the end of the red underground line in 'Lowtown', he trained in Birmingham as an actor and singer, later enjoying several years in the professional theatre, both in the provinces and in London's West End. A lifetime's love of classical music eventually found him at the old store in Oxford Street at HMV. Computers were still in their infancy, therefore an encyclopaedic knowledge of recordings was a must. Other jobs have followed and the need to write/scribble has always been there. Oh to be organized!

Enter Bing, and his enquiring mind. The journey continues...

If you've enjoyed
The Ruminations of Bing,
check out
The Meanderings of Bing
and
The Ramblings of Bing

About the Publishers

Saron Publishers has been in existence for about fourteen years, producing niche magazines. Our first venture into books took place in 2016 when we published *The Meanderings of Bing* by Tim Harnden-Taylor. Further publications include *Minstrel Magic,* by Eleanor Pritchard, George Mitchell's biography, *Penthusiasm,* a collection of short stories and poems from Penthusiasts, a writing group based in the beautiful town of Usk, and *Frank,* a gentle novel about loss, by Julie Hamill. Its sequel *Jackie* will be out later in 2019.

2019 will also see the publication of Darcy Drummond's third novel, *High Manor,* following the successful *Summer Season* and *Water of Life.* Kevin Moore's second book, *Real Murder Investigations – An Insider's View,* delves in more detail into some cases mentioned in his previous book, *My Way.*

Why not join our mailing list by emailing info@saronpublishers.co.uk. We promise no spam ever.

Visit our website saronpublishers.co.uk to keep up to date and to read reviews of what we've been reading and enjoying. You can also enjoy the occasional offer of a free Bing chapter.

Follow us on Facebook @saronpublishing.

Follow us on Twitter @saronpublishers.

www.ingramcontent.com/pod-product-compliance
Lightning Source LLC
Chambersburg PA
CBHW060358080526
44583CB00012B/378